Tradition

Tradition

Understanding Christian Tradition

GERALD O'COLLINS, SJ

OXFORD
UNIVERSITY PRESS

OXFORD
UNIVERSITY PRESS

Great Clarendon Street, Oxford, OX2 6DP,
United Kingdom

Oxford University Press is a department of the University of Oxford.
It furthers the University's objective of excellence in research, scholarship,
and education by publishing worldwide. Oxford is a registered trade mark of
Oxford University Press in the UK and in certain other countries

© Gerald O'Collins, SJ 2018

The moral rights of the author have been asserted

First Edition published in 2018

Impression: 1

Published in the United States of America by Oxford University Press
198 Madison Avenue, New York, NY 10016, United States of America

British Library Cataloguing in Publication Data
Data available

Library of Congress Control Number: 2018939609

ISBN 978–0–19–883030–6

Printed and bound in Great Britain by
Clays Ltd, Elcograf S.p.A.

Preface

Recently I received an invitation to the launch of a book entitled *Educating for Purposeful Living in a Post-Traditional Age*. A prior engagement prevented me from accepting the invitation. If I had been able to attend the launch, I would have questioned the author over the place of 'post-traditional' in his title.

Did he mean that we are living in an age which has abandoned many long established customs and practices? That is uncontroversial and obviously true. Many traditional views and values have been judged to be outdated and dropped. With the authority of tradition widely disputed, one cannot appeal to the grounds that 'this is the way it has always been' and 'this is the way it should remain'. But did the author of *Living in a Post-Traditional Age* mean that our age has literally moved beyond all tradition, and is post-traditional in the extreme sense of having given up its entire heritage? Such a total break with tradition is neither desirable nor possible.

Learning a language, for instance, involves learning a tradition. Every language, even a language open to remarkable change, is traditional. As it is handed on through teaching and learning, it acts as a major tradition by providing group cohesion and exercising a measure of social control. Paradoxically those who speak out against tradition do so through their inherited language. They use traditional language to challenge tradition.

To allege that we live in a 'post-traditional age' can be as confusing as alleging that we live in a 'post-historical age'. Even those who prefer to remain largely unaware of their historical heritage have been shaped, individually and collectively, by history. Consciously or, much more frequently, unconsciously we may take our history in new directions. But a total break with our inherited history remains as impossible as a total break with the tradition we have inherited in so many fields. Tradition, whether recent or older, remains present in every field of human existence and endeavour.

Those who pit modernity against tradition risk forgetting that some tradition or traditions may in fact provide the direction for a valuable renewal. It was precisely through retrieving teaching from Thomas Aquinas and even earlier traditions that Pope Francis reformed the situation of the Eucharist being denied to the divorced and civilly remarried who are sexually active. His 2016 exhortation *Amoris Laetitia* (the Joy of Love) that signalled this change will be examined later. Here let me simply cite this reform as an example of tradition proving productive and bringing life-giving change. The new drew its inspiration from the old.

Right from the outset, it is important to alert readers to the way 'tradition' may designate either a process (the act of handing on, *actus tradendi*, *traditio activa*) or what is handed on (the object or content, *traditum*, *traditio passiva*). Where English has at its disposal only one word 'tradition', German enjoys two words: *Überlieferung* and *Tradition*. The former tends to suggest the act of handing on, while the latter tends to suggest the object that is handed on. Even so, there is no hard and fast distinction in German usage of the two terms. In this book the context should make it clear which meaning is intended when we speak of 'tradition': either the act of transmission or the content of what is transmitted. We would waste time to explain constantly whether it is the process or the content that is intended.

This book begins with positions on tradition that many Christians came to share in the second half of the twentieth century (Chapter 1). A real, if incomplete, convergence on tradition shows up when we compare a 1963 report from the Faith and Order Commission of the World Council of Churches with a 1965 document expounding tradition published by the Second Vatican Council. Our first chapter presents this convergence.

For years biblical scholars have used sociology and other social sciences to advantage in illuminating the biblical traditions—something noted with approval in the Pontifical Biblical Commission's *The Interpretation of the Bible in the Church* (Rome: Libreria Editrice Vaticana, 1993, 57–63). The few theologians who have in recent years written about Christian tradition (see the entries in my bibliography for D. Brown, S. R. Holmes, H. J. Pottmeyer, J. E. Thiel, and D. H. Williams) have drawn nothing from sociological insights into the role of tradition in human and religious life. They have regularly neglected the help towards understanding tradition which they might have received from Peter Berger, Anthony Giddens, Edward Shils, and other experts in the social sciences. What difference does tradition make in human life? Chapter 2 will cite answers coming, above all, from sociologists and promising to shed valuable light on the religious tradition of Christians. It will set out, in particular, four positions developed by Shils.

In the light of the divine self-revelation that reached its highpoint through Christ and the New Testament Church, Chapter 3 will lay out seven characteristics of Christian 'tradition', and present the crucified and risen Jesus (the *Christus praesens*) as the central *Traditum*. It will also examine the language of 'culture'. While closely associated with 'tradition', 'culture' is not identical and should not be taken as a substitute.

All the baptized play at least some minimal role in transmitting tradition, and can do so in indefinitely many ways. Chapter 4 will examine (a) the 'transmitters' of tradition, (b) the 'sense of the faithful' (*sensus fidelium*) that inspires their handing on of tradition, and (c) the role of official teachers in the transmission of tradition. A 'sense of tradition' (*sensus traditionis*) is shared, at least minimally, by all Christians. The essential, if invisible, agent of tradition remains always the Holy Spirit.

Chapter 5 moves to the mutual dependence of Scripture and tradition. To illustrate this dependence, it reflects on three examples: the emergence of the creeds, the development of the image of Christ as the New or Last Adam, and the doctrine of justification. The chapter then focuses on the role of Scripture in reforming long-standing teaching on religious freedom and combating scandalous anti-Semitism. It is within the full context of Christian life and history that we should reflect on the relationship between Scripture and tradition.

Chapter 6 will face the constant challenge (coming, for instance, from pastoral leaders, biblical scholars, and others) that calls for existing Christian traditions to be discerned and possibly reformed. The chapter also considers the need to evaluate cultural traditions in Africa, Asia, Latin America, and elsewhere that can or should have their part when inculturating the good news of Christ. What principles should come into play in all this discerning and evaluating?

Chapter 7 will sum up the conclusions and major achievements of this book. Finally, by showing how modern memory studies illuminate significantly the nature of Christian tradition, an appendix will add to what Chapter 2 has already drawn from the social sciences. The appendix illustrates further the failure of theologies of tradition to profit from the social studies—in this case, from memory studies that have flourished for decades. Biblical scholars have drawn on those studies, right down to S. Butticaz and E. Norelli (eds), *Memory and Memories in Early Christianity* (Tübingen: Mohr Siebeck, 2018).

By presenting Christian tradition, this book completes a trilogy— on revelation (*Revelation: Towards a Christian Interpretation of God's Self-Revelation in Jesus Christ* (Oxford University Press, 2016)), tradition, and Sacred Scripture (*Towards a Christian Interpretation of Biblical Inspiration* (Oxford University Press, 2018)). I wish to thank Tom Perridge, Karen Raith, the delegates of Oxford University Press, and two anonymous readers for accepting this book. My warm thanks also go to David Braithwaite, Brendan Byrne, Joshua Choong, Isaac Demase, Massimo Faggioli, Anne Hunt, Robin Koning, Jack Otto, Jin-hyuk Park, Ormond Rush, Tan Tran, Sabine Voermans, Denis White, and Jared Wicks for various kinds of help towards creating this study on tradition.

The book seems necessary, given the way theologians currently neglect the theme of Christian tradition. The *New Dictionary of Theology*, ed. M. Davie et al., 2nd edn (Downer's Grove, IL: Inter-Varsity Press, 2016) provides a startling case of such neglect. This large dictionary contains no entry on 'Tradition', and does not even list 'tradition' in its index.

With great esteem and affection, I dedicate this book to the memory of René Latourelle (1918–2017), twelve years dean of theology at the Gregorian University (Rome) and a pervasive influence in my theological life. When quoting the Bible, I normally follow the New Revised Standard Version (NRSV); the translations from the Latin texts of the Second Vatican Council (1962–5) are my own. As a Christian, I use the terminology of the Old Testament and the New Testament. Here 'old' is understood as 'good' and does not imply 'supersessionism', or the view that the New Testament has rendered obsolete and so superseded the Old Testament.

Australian Catholic University and University
of Divinity (Melbourne),
Pentecost Sunday, 2018
Gerald O'Collins, SJ, AC

Contents

List of Abbreviations

ABD　　　　D. N. Freedman (ed.), *Anchor Bible Dictionary*, 6 vols
　　　　　　(New York: Doubleday, 1992).

AG　　　　Second Vatican Council, *Ad Gentes* (Decree on the
　　　　　　Church's Missionary Activity), 1965.

Bettenson　H. Bettenson and C. Maunder, *Documents of the Christian
　　　　　　Church*, 4th edn (Oxford: Oxford University Press, 2011).

DH　　　　Second Vatican Council, *Dignitatis Humanae* (Declaration
　　　　　　on Religious Liberty), 1965.

DV　　　　Second Vatican Council, *Dei Verbum* (Constitution on
　　　　　　Divine Revelation), 1965.

DzH　　　　H. Denzinger and P. Hünermann (eds), *Enchiridion
　　　　　　symbolorum, definitionum et declarationum*, English trans.,
　　　　　　43rd edn (San Francisco: Ignatius Press, 2012).

FC　　　　John Paul II, *Familiaris Consortio* (Apostolic Exhortation on
　　　　　　the Role of the Christian Family in the Modern World),
　　　　　　1981.

GS　　　　Second Vatican Council, *Gaudium et Spes* (Constitution on
　　　　　　the Church in the Modern World), 1965.

HFTh　　　W. Kern, H. J. Pottmeyer, and M. Seckler (eds), *Handbuch
　　　　　　der Fundamentaltheologie*, 4 vols (Freiburg im Breisgau:
　　　　　　Herder, 1985–8).

LG　　　　Second Vatican Council, *Lumen Gentium* (Constitution on
　　　　　　the Church), 1964.

Montreal 63　Faith and Order Commission, *The Fourth World Conference
　　　　　　on Faith and Order, Montreal 1963*.

NA　　　　Second Vatican Council, *Nostra Aetate* (Declaration on the
　　　　　　Relation of the Church to Non-Christian Religions), 1965.

ND　　　　J. Neuner and J. Dupuis (eds), *The Christian Faith*, 7th edn
　　　　　　(Bangalore: Theological Publications in India, 2001).

par (r).　　parallel(s) in other Gospels.

PL　　　　*Patrologia Latina*, ed. J. P. Migne, 221 vols (Paris, 1844–64).

SC   Second Vatican Council, *Sacrosanctum Concilium*
            (Constitution on the Sacred Liturgy), 1963.

TRE   G. Krause and G. Müller (eds), *Theologische Realenzyklopädie*,
            36 vols (Berlin: Walter de Gruyter, 1977–2004).

UR   Second Vatican Council, *Unitatis Redintegratio* (Decree on
            Ecumenism), 1964.

1

The Background for Discussing Christian Tradition

On the eve of the Second Vatican Council (1962–5), James Mackey published *The Modern Theology of Tradition*, a work which became a classic in its field. He proposed that a modern theology of tradition should begin with Johannes Baptist Franzelin (1816–86), a papal theologian at the First Vatican Council (1869–70).[1] He had, nevertheless, to present the background to this theology in the Council of Trent's response to the Reformation principle of *sola Scriptura* (Scripture alone)—a response which, right down to Vatican II, was regularly misunderstood as alleging 'two sources' of revelation (Scripture and tradition).[2] Before moving to Trent, we must ask: What did Protestants mean by *sola Scriptura*?

'Scripture Alone', and Trent on Tradition

The explosion of publications that followed Johannes Gutenberg's invention of the printing press around 1450 promoted the humanist renaissance, which numbered many Reformers among its leaders. Excitement over the Scriptures and their message of grace, forgiveness, and freedom joined forces with a vigorous reaction against decadent traditions and various commandments of the Church. The Reformers, when they rediscovered central themes of the New Testament, turned against such human enactments as the laws of fasting, the rule of annual

---

[1] J. B. Franzelin, *De Divina Traditione et Scriptura*, 4th edn (Rome: Typografia Polyglotta S.C. de Propaganda Fide, 1896). See J. P. Mackey, *The Modern Theology of Tradition* (London: Darton, Longman & Todd, 1962), 5–52.

[2] Mackey, *The Modern Theology of Tradition*, 8, 14, 51, 150–9, 180–1.

confession, the practice of indulgences, and the obligation of celibacy for religious and Latin-rite priests. Understanding the Bible and not human traditions to be the only authoritative rule for faith, Luther made *sola Scriptura* a battle cry in his campaign to reform the Catholic Church.

The main thrust of the principle could be put as follows. Within the limits of the biblical text, the Holy Spirit actively expresses the truth of revelation and brings into play the saving reality of Jesus Christ. The Bible alone exercises the role of being the exclusive rule of faith. A 1963 conference of the Faith and Order Commission (the theological think-tank of the World Council of Churches) sums up the scope of *sola Scriptura* this way: 'The Protestant position has been an appeal to Holy Scripture alone, as the infallible and sufficient authority in all matters pertaining to salvation, to which all human traditions should be subjected.'[3]

In its decree of 8 April 1546 (Bettenson 275–6; DzH 1501–9; ND 210–15), the Council of Trent did not intend to give a complete exposé of tradition but wished to correct 'the Scripture alone' principle of the Reformers.[4] After acknowledging 'the Gospel (*evangelium*)', which we can unpack as the original or 'foundational' revelation completed with Jesus Christ, to be 'the source [singular] of all saving truth and [all] regulation of conduct', Trent pointed to the written books of the Bible and the unwritten (apostolic) traditions (plural) as 'containing' this truth and regulation.[5] Against attempts to make the Bible the only guide to divine revelation and human faith, the Council maintained that the Church's tradition also preserved and disclosed 'the Gospel'. Hence we can expect to find revelation expressed,

---

[3] P. C. Rodger and L. Vischer (eds), 'The Report of the Theological Commission on "Tradition and Traditions"', *The Fourth World Conference on Faith and Order, Montreal 1963* (London: SCM Press, 1963), 3–63, at 51; hereafter *Montreal 63*. On this study, see B. Gaybba, *The Tradition: An Ecumenical Breakthrough? (A Study of a Faith and Order Study)* (Rome: Herder, 1971).

[4] See T. Rasmussen, 'Tradition', in H. J. Hillerbrand (ed.), *The Oxford Encyclopedia of the Reformation*, iv (New York: Oxford University Press, 1996), 166–9; J. W. O'Malley, *Trent: What Happened at the Council* (Cambridge, MA: Belknap Press of Harvard University Press, 2013), 92–3, 97–8, 304–5.

[5] The translation of the decree is my own.

recorded, and actualized through various traditions, as well as through the inspired Scriptures.[6]

The decree of Trent suffered from (a) inappropriate language and (b) subsequent misinterpretation. (a) As we have just seen, the Council spoke of 'all saving truth and [all] regulation of conduct' being '*contained*' in the inspired Scriptures and 'unwritten [apostolic] traditions' (emphasis added). So long as Catholic theologians (like many of their Protestant counterparts)[7] endorsed a propositional view of revelation as God manifesting certain (hitherto undisclosed) truths, they remained comfortable with such language. They were concerned to establish where various revealed truths were 'contained' and to be found. From a 'quantitative' point of view, they could raise the question: even if the Bible is not 'formally sufficient' (inasmuch as it needs to be interpreted by tradition), is it 'materially sufficient' in communicating the truths (plural) of revelation? Does it 'contain' all the truths? Or are some truths (e.g. the immaculate conception and bodily assumption of the Blessed Virgin Mary) 'contained' only in tradition?

Juxtaposing Scripture and tradition in this 'material' way degraded tradition and revelation—not to mention Scripture itself. Tradition became a mere vehicle for carrying revealed contents, and precisely as such turned into something extrinsic to revelation. Revelation then sounded like something to be transported from one generation to the next. After the apostolic generation (which had received all the truths of revelation but did not record all of them in the inspired Scriptures) had died out, later Christians, it was argued, had the duty of handing on through tradition the full list of revealed truths. Faithful tradition, as well as the preservation of the Bible, enabled the Church to retain all the truths revealed at the foundation of Christianity.

(b) Theologians read Trent's decree as if it taught two 'materially' separate and equally valid 'sources' (plural) of revelation, one being Scripture and the other being tradition. In a series of studies, however, a Tübingen theologian, Josef Rupert Geiselmann (1890–1970), even if

[6] On the decree of Trent, see J. E. Thiel, *Senses of Tradition: Continuity and Development in Catholic Faith* (New York: Oxford University Press, 2000), 17–25.

[7] See G. O'Collins, *Revelation: Towards a Christian Interpretation of God's Self-Revelation in Jesus Christ* (Oxford: Oxford University Press, 2016), 4–5.

some details of his case had to be corrected, established that the 'two-source' theory could not claim support from Trent. The Council reserved the term 'source' exclusively for 'the Gospel' or the one revealed message of salvation embodied in and communicated by Christ.[8]

But prior to the work of Geiselmann, the 'two-source' theory was standard in Catholic theology. Even worse, through the nineteenth century not only Franzelin but more and more theologians tended to identify tradition with the magisterium or teaching office of the pope and bishops.[9] Pushed to its logical conclusion, this view of tradition and its witnesses would lead to the words allegedly spoken by Pope Pius IX on 19 June 1870: 'Witnesses to tradition? There is only one witness, myself.'[10]

Yet, the same nineteenth century also saw some healthier development of views on tradition, both in itself and in its relationship to Scripture. Members of the 'Tübingen School', Johann Sebastian Drey (1777–1853) and Johann Adam Möhler (1796–1838), interpreted tradition as 'living tradition', and Möhler introduced an organic model in presenting tradition.[11] Geiselmann was to use 'living tradition' for the title of one of his key works: *Die lebendige Überlieferung als Norm der christlichen Glaubens* (Living Tradition as Norm of Christian

---

[8] J. R. Geiselmann, 'Un malentendu éclairci: La relation "Écriture-tradition" dans la théologie catholique', *Istina* 5 (1958), 197–214; the German original of this article appeared in *Una Sancta* 11 (1956), 131–50; Geiselmann, 'Das Konzil von Trient über das Verhältnis der Heiligen Schrift und der nicht geschriebenen Traditionen. Sein Missverständnis in der nachtridentinischen Theologie und die Überwindung dieses Missverständnisses', in M. Schmaus (ed.), *Die mündliche Überlieferung: Beiträge zum Begriff der Tradition* (Munich: Max Hüber Verlag, 1957), 123–206; Geiselmann, *Die heilige Schrift und die Tradition* (Freiburg im Breisgau: Herder, 1962). See P. de Voogt, 'Écriture et tradition d'après des études catholique récentes', *Istina* 5 (1958), 183–96; W. Pannenberg, *Systematic Theology*, trans. G. W. Bromiley, i (Grand Rapids, MI: Eerdmans, 1991), 26–33; J. Ratzinger, in K. Rahner and J. Ratzinger, *Revelation and Tradition*, trans. W. J. O'Hara (London: Burns & Oates, 1966), 50–68.

[9] See Mackey, *The Modern Theology of Tradition*, 1–52; W. Kasper, *Die Lehre der Tradition in der Römischen Schule* (Freiburg im Breisgau: Herder, 1962).

[10] J. R. Geiselmann, *The Meaning of Tradition*, trans. W. J. O'Hara (New York: Herder and Herder, 1966; German orig. 1962), 16, 113–14.

[11] Thiel, *Senses of Tradition*, 59–67; Geiselmann, *The Meaning of Tradition*, 49–73.

Faith).[12] Less than ten years later the Second Vatican Council's Constitution on Divine Revelation paid tribute to those who had elaborated the notion of 'living tradition', by teaching that, when elucidating the meaning of the Sacred Scriptures, readers should take into account 'the living Tradition of the whole Church' (*DV* 12). Sadly the translation of the Vatican II documents edited by Austin Flannery, even in its 1988 revised edition, omitted 'living' and simply rendered the phrase as 'the Tradition of the entire Church'.[13] A courteous and grateful nod towards the Tübingen School was lost.

As we saw, a propositional view of revelation lay behind the typical Catholic, post-Council of Trent understanding of tradition and the tradition–Scripture issue. When a shift eventually came to an inter-personal model of revelation, this put in first place the self-revelation of God. Revelation is something that happens—a living encounter with the personal reality of God; it is not, properly speaking, described as being 'contained' in anything, whether it be Scripture or tradition. A hint of such a shift came at the First Vatican Council in its constitution on faith, which placed its primary emphasis on the super-natural disclosure of new truths that significantly enrich our know-ledge of God, with the act of faith as an assent to these truths or believing 'the things' to be true that God has revealed (DzH 3008; ND 118). Nevertheless, in passing, Vatican I did speak more personally of divine revelation as God being 'pleased *to reveal himself* and his eternal decrees' (DzH 3004; ND 113; emphasis added). The opening chapter of Vatican II's Constitution on Divine Revelation makes it abundantly clear that revelation primarily means God's personal self-revelation that elicits human faith (*DV* 1–4). In a second-ary sense, revelation encompasses the truths which are now disclosed about God and human beings. (We return to this question in Chapter 3 below.)

Protestant theologians were quicker off the mark in presenting revelation as primarily the self-disclosure of God. Wilhelm Hermann (1846–1922), a German Lutheran, firmly stated in his 1887 work, *Der Begriff der Offenbarung* (The Notion of Revelation): 'all revelation is the

---

[12] (Freiburg im Breisgau: Herder, 1959).
[13] (Northport, NY: Costello, 1988), 758.

self-revelation of God'.[14] Wolfhart Pannenberg named Friedrich Schelling (1775–1854) as the scholar who introduced the expression 'self-revelation' into modern theology and philosophy, but traced the origins of the notion back to Philo and Plotinus.[15]

Protestant Changes on Tradition

By the time the Fourth World Conference of Faith and Order met in Montreal in the summer of 1963, a sea change had taken place in much Protestant thinking about tradition and its relationship to Scripture. From the sixteenth century, the *sola Scriptura* view that the Bible by itself should determine Christian faith and practice was challenged. To begin with, the Bible itself nowhere claims to function, independently of tradition, as if it were the exclusive norm of faith. Substantially the product of Jewish and apostolic traditions, the Bible could never have come into existence without them. Since, through the inspiration of the Holy Spirit, the community's tradition led to the formation of the Sacred Scriptures, one would expect tradition to remain active in interpreting and applying the Scriptures and in evoking and guiding the response of faith.

The overwhelming majority of Protestant Reformers never in fact drew their belief and practice solely from their experience of the Scriptures. Thus nearly all the Reformers maintained, for instance, the traditional belief in the Blessed Trinity, even though a properly articulated doctrine of the Trinity was worked out only at two fourth-century councils, Nicaea I and Constantinople I. Moreover, most Protestants did not appeal to the *sola Scriptura* principle and abandon infant baptism, a practice which does not enjoy a clear and compelling warrant in the New Testament.

Tradition retained its normativity, albeit a subordinate normativity. In 'Scripture', Richard Muller writes, 'neither the reformers nor

---

[14] Quoted by J. Baillie, *The Idea of Revelation in Recent Thought* (London: Oxford University Press, 1956), 34.

[15] Pannenberg also cited Aquinas, Bonaventure, Cajetan, and Hegel as proposing divine self-revelation, even if they did not use the precise term; see 'Offenbarung und "Offenbarungen" im Zeugnis der Geschichte', in *HFTh*, ii, 63–82.

their successors sought to reject the Church's tradition'. In fact, 'virtually all the Protestant confessions of the sixteenth century indicate the normative character, subordinate to Scripture, of the ecumenical creeds of the Church'.[16]

The difficulty of basing belief and practice simply on the Scriptures became even more acute when modern biblical studies began in the late seventeenth century with the critical work of such writers as Richard Simon (1638–1712). Scholars began recognizing that more than one author was involved in making the Pentateuch; not everything attributed to Moses was written by him. A chronology and understanding of world history based on the Bible were rendered obsolete. Biblical studies turned 'scientific'; the Enlightenment encouraged the quest for a rational religion and the rejection of Jesus' resurrection (Hermann Samuel Reimarus, 1694–1768). David Friedrich Strauss (1808–74) interpreted the Gospels as myths. Throughout the nineteenth century, liberal Christians or straight non-believers produced their lives of Jesus, representing him merely as a moral reformer or human teacher of wisdom. They used historical data to undercut orthodox faith in the divine-human Christ of the Church's creeds.[17] An even more serious challenge came from the history of religions school that arose at the end of the nineteenth century. Led by such scholars as Wilhelm Bousset (1865–1920), this group drew from comparative religion with a view to minimalizing the claims of the New Testament and the importance of Christian doctrines.[18]

In general, exegetes confined the sense of Scriptures to their strictly literal meaning and reconstructed the prehistory of these texts. It became more problematic to support Christian faith and practice simply and solely on the basis of the Scriptures. Which learned professor should one follow in acknowledging the 'literal' meaning or reconstructing the genesis of given biblical texts?

[16] R. A. Muller, 'Scripture', *Oxford Encyclopedia of the Reformation*, iv, 36–9, at 36.

[17] Albert Schweitzer told the story brilliantly: *The Quest of the Historical Jesus*, trans. W. Montgomery, 2nd edn (London: A. & C. Black 1936; German orig. 1906).

[18] See W. A. Meeks, 'The History of Religions School', in J. Riches (ed.), *The New Cambridge History of the Bible: From 1750 to the Present*, iv (Cambridge: Cambridge University Press, 2015), 127–38.

Add to this the challenge coming from modern hermeneutics or theories about the right methods for interpreting scriptural and other texts, launched by F. D. E. Schleiermacher (1768–1834) and developed by Wilhelm Dilthey (1833–1911).[19] Do we understand texts by seeking to recreate the intentions of the author(s)? Or can texts mean something more than what the historical authors consciously intended? What theory of hermeneutics should one follow? The rise of modern biblical scholarship and hermeneutics has made easy appeals to the 'plain sense' of the Scriptures problematic.[20]

Some Protestant authors have at times considered whether by itself the Bible brings multiplicity and division rather than unity.[21] If the biblical texts agreed on more than they do and if their literal meaning emerged with mathematical clarity, the Scriptures might have effected agreement in expressing substantially the Christian experience of the divine self-communication. But the books of the biblical canon, while converging frequently, can also differ strikingly. As for their meaning, we *create*, as well as *discover*, meaning when we read biblical and other texts. Not only public contexts but also what individuals bring to the reading or hearing of the Scriptures (their deep questions, previous experiences, inherited assumptions, actual commitments, and personal history) affects the meanings they proceed to champion. Right from the early centuries of Christianity, protagonists of division and even of such heresies as Arianism have supported their interpretation of the divine self-revelation by appeals to the Scriptures. The verdict of history seems clear. The principle of *sola Scriptura*, if taken strictly, can hardly promise to bring easy agreement about right ways to interpret, express, and live out the experience of God's self-disclosure in Christ.

[19] See W. G. Jeanrond, 'Interpretation, History of', *ABD*, iii, 424–43; Jeanrond, 'The Bible in Philosophy and Hermeneutics', *The New Cambridge History of the Bible*, iv, 314–27; B. C. Lategan, 'Hermeneutics', *ABD*, iii, 149–55; A. C. Thiselton, *Hermeneutics: An Introduction* (Grand Rapids, MI: Eerdmans, 2009).

[20] On the 'plain sense', see Thiel, *Senses of Tradition*, 34–9.

[21] E. Käsemann, 'Unity and Multiplicity in the New Testament Doctrine of the Church', *New Testament Questions of Today*, trans. W. J. Montague (London: SCM Press, 1969; German orig. 1963), 252–9.

Moreover, it seems too much to expect the Scriptures by themselves to provide answers, especially full and convincing ones, to new challenges. Faced with the new questions, unexpected problems, and whole medley of fresh experiences that characterize the modern world, how should we interpret and express the foundational experience of God's self-communication that the Scriptures have recorded and interpreted? More briefly, how could the Bible by itself respond to issues that arose only after the close of the apostolic age? For instance, a Greek philosophical mindset raised questions about the 'person' and 'natures' of Christ that the New Testament could not be expected to answer clearly. The authors of the New Testament and the traditions they drew on did not face such issues, and hence could hardly be expected by themselves to yield the appropriate answers. These questions touched something utterly basic—the right way to discern, interpret, and express what or rather whom the first disciples had experienced in the life, death, and resurrection of Jesus Christ, along with the coming of the Holy Spirit. The questions were crucial, but the New Testament by itself could not readily give the answers.

By the middle of the twentieth century, such leading Lutheran scholars as Gerhard Ebeling (1912–2001) reflected a shift in views on Scripture and tradition. When maintaining that proclamation is the proper task of theology, he stated that theology should also be concerned with 'the proclamation that has already taken place' and wrote: 'the task which theology is given to do is identical with the gift it receives from tradition'. Hence 'the task of handing on this tradition . . . is clearly constitutive of theology'.[22] In a long essay '*Sola Scriptura* and Tradition', which he prepared for the 1963 Faith and Order conference in Montreal, he admitted: 'the Scripture principle necessarily involves a doctrine of tradition'.[23]

The classic theological work of Paul Tillich also signalled a change towards expressly appreciating the role of tradition. He presented

---

[22] G. Ebeling, *Theology and Proclamation*, trans. J. Riches (London: Collins, 1966; German orig. 1962), 22–3; see also 15–16, 25–31.

[23] G. Ebeling, *The Word of God and Tradition*, trans. S. H. Hooke (London: Collins, 1968; German orig. 1964), 102–47, at 144.

tradition as an indispensable feature of human and Christian life.[24] Ernst Käsemann, a prominent Lutheran exegete, in a lecture on 'Unity and Multiplicity in the New Testament Doctrine of the Church', reflected this new appreciation of tradition: '[the Holy] Spirit and tradition must not be identified, *but neither are they mutually exclusive*'.[25]

The change that occurred was partly due to the hermeneutical views of Hans-Georg Gadamer (1900–2002). This Protestant philosopher incorporated tradition into interpretation, explaining it not as an obstacle but as a necessary context for the recovery of meaning. Tradition 'is the way we relate to the past' or the way the past is present. Hence 'we are always situated within traditions'; tradition 'is always part of us'.[26] Wolfhart Pannenberg (1928–2014), in a long study, 'A Methodology for Understanding Meaning', reflects the significance of Gadamer through his positive attitude towards the principle of tradition.[27]

The 1963 Faith and Order Conference in Montreal

In *The Tradition: An Ecumenical Breakthrough*, Brian Gaybba has provided a useful account of the work of a commission, formed a year after the

---

[24] P. Tillich, *Systematic Theology*, iii (Chicago: University of Chicago Press, 1963), 183–5.

[25] Käsemann, *New Testament Questions of Today*, 252–9, at 256; emphasis added.

[26] H.-G. Gadamer, *Truth and Method*, trans. J. Weinsheimer and D. G. Marshall, 2nd edn (New York: Crossroad, 1992; German orig. 1960), 282. In his essay 'Sola Scriptura and Tradition', Ebeling twice cites Gadamer (240, 251–2). Both Ebeling and Gadamer contributed to 'Tradition', in K. Galling et al. (eds), *Die Religion in Geschichte und Gegenwart*, 3rd edn, vi (Tübingen: Mohr Siebeck, 1962), 966–84.

[27] W. Pannenberg, *Theology and the Philosophy of Science*, trans. F. McDonagh (London: Darton, Longman & Todd, 1976; German orig. 1973), 156–224, esp. 197–8; see also Pannenberg, 'The Crisis of the Scripture Principle', *Basic Questions in Theology*, trans. G. H. Kehm, i (London: SCM Press, 1974; German orig. 1962), 1–14. On the place of tradition in modern Protestant theology, see Y. Congar, *Tradition and Traditions: An Historical and Theological Essay*, trans. M. Naseby and T. Rainborough (London: Burns & Oates, 1966; French orig. 1960 and 1963), 459–82. Congar may have taken the title *Tradition and Traditions* from the project assigned by the Faith and Order Commission in 1953 to the new commission on 'Tradition and Traditions'.

Third World Conference of the World Council of Churches' Faith
and Order Commission had met in Lund in 1952. The 1953 commission, with a European and a North American section, was given
the task of studying 'Tradition and Traditions'. Ebeling became a
member of the European section of the commission in 1955. Ten
years of work by this commission culminated in a report on the subject
issued by the Fourth World Conference of Faith and Order in 1963.[28]
This Montreal report anticipated several lines of Catholic reflection
on tradition, which were to be incorporated in a Vatican II document
of 1965, *Dei Verbum*.

Some of what was endorsed in Montreal and Rome echoed the
findings of Yves Congar (1904–95), above all his magisterial *Tradition
and Traditions*, which originally appeared in French in two volumes
(1960 and 1963).[29] In view of the coming Montreal conference (July
1963), the Bossey Ecumenical Institute (funded and run by the World
Council of Churches) hosted a consultation between the Faith and
Order Commission and the Catholic Conference for Ecumenical
Affairs (18–23 March 1963), and discussed reports prepared for
Montreal. Congar attended and commented on a key report, entitled
'Tradition and Traditions'.[30] Involved in work for Vatican II, he
could not attend the Montreal conference. But he had already made
his contribution to that conference through the Bossey consultation
and, previously, in other ways. The leading *peritus* (theological expert)
at Vatican II, he had a hand in drafting eight out of the sixteen
documents, including *Dei Verbum* and, specifically, its Chapter 2 (on
tradition). Let me signal seven lines of convergence between *Dei
Verbum* and the Montreal report.

Firstly, the *model of revelation* as divine self-communication was
decisive for the Montreal report and *Dei Verbum*. Since it was agreed
that revelation is *primarily* a personal encounter with God (who is

---

[28] See Gaybba, *The Tradition: An Ecumenical Breakthrough?*; and J. G. Boeglin, *La
question de la tradition dans la théologie catholique contemporaine* (Paris: Cerf, 1998),
250–70.

[29] See also Y. Congar, *Tradition and the Life of the Church*, trans. A. N. Woodrow
(London: Burns & Oates, 1964; French orig. 1963).

[30] See Y. Congar, *My Journal of the Council*, trans. M. J. Ronayne and
M. C. Boulding (Collegeville, MN: Liturgical Press, 2012), 283–5.

Truth) rather than the communication of a body of hitherto unknown truths, the heat went out of any 'quantitative' debate about some revealed truths being 'contained' in Scripture and others being possibly 'contained' only in tradition.

The Montreal conference stated: 'as Christians, we all acknowledge with thankfulness that God *has revealed himself* in the history of the people of God in the Old Testament, and in Christ Jesus, his Son, the mediator between God and man [*sic*]'.[31] The opening chapter of Vatican II's Constitution on Divine Revelation repeatedly clarified its primary meaning as divine self-disclosure: 'it pleased God in his goodness and wisdom to reveal himself'; 'Christ himself is both the mediator and fullness of all revelation' (*DV* 2); 'by divine revelation God wished to manifest and communicate both himself and the eternal decrees of his will concerning the salvation of human kind' (*DV* 6).[32]

This personal understanding of revelation underpinned what happened when the Faith and Order Commission and Vatican II connected revelation, tradition, and inspired Scriptures—in that order. Testimony to the divine self-revelation on the part of the Old Testament prophets (understood in a broad sense) and the New Testament apostles (likewise understood in a broad sense) inaugurated the tradition. Then, in the words of the Faith and Order Commission, 'the oral and written tradition of the prophets and apostles under the guidance of the Holy Spirit led to the formation of Scriptures and to the canonization of the Old and New Testaments as the Bible of the Church'.[33] The same order fashioned *Dei Verbum*: revelation (Ch. 1), tradition (Ch. 2), and the Scriptures (Chs 3–6).

Second, both the Montreal document and *Dei Verbum* embodied 'total' views of tradition as being the whole *living heritage* which is passed on. *Dei Verbum* declared: 'What was handed on by the Apostles includes *everything* that contributes to making the People of God live their life in holiness and grow in faith. In this way, the Church, in her doctrine, life, and worship, perpetuates and transmits to all

---

[31] *Montreal 1963*, 51.

[32] See J. Wicks, 'The Fullness of Revelation in Christ in *Dei Verbum*', *Gregorianum* 99 (2018), forthcoming.

[33] *Montreal 1963*, 51.

generations *everything* that she herself is, *everything* that she believes' (*DV* 9; emphasis added). The Montreal report likewise described Tradition in global terms as 'the Gospel itself, transmitted from generation to generation in and by the Church'.[34]

The Gospel (or apostolic Tradition (with a capital T)) is ultimately not merely the good news *about* Jesus Christ but *is* Jesus Christ (see Mark 1: 1, 14–15). Hence the Montreal report leaned towards interpreting the essential *Traditum* (or what is handed on) as 'Christ himself present in the life of the Church'.[35] It preferred to move beneath the *visible* human realities which make up the Christian life of faith and emphasize the *invisible* reality of the risen Christ present among believers. That presence constitutes the heart of the *Traditum*: 'what is transmitted in the process of tradition is the Christian faith, not only as a sum of tenets [equivalent to 'everything that she [the Church] believes' of *DV* 8] but [also] as a living reality transmitted through the operation of the Holy Spirit. We can speak of the Christian Tradition (with a capital T), whose content [*sic*] is God's revelation and self-giving in Christ, present in the life of the Church'.[36]

The Montreal document drew the appropriate conclusion from its interpretation of tradition as *Christus praesens*: 'the Tradition of the Church is not an object which we *possess* but a reality by which we *are possessed*'.[37] More than merely the visible sum of beliefs and practices which Christians hand on, Tradition (upper case) is the saving presence of the risen Christ, engaged in a process of self-transmission through the Holy Spirit in the ongoing life of the Church.[38]

---

[34] Ibid. 50.

[35] Ibid. This echoes the final sentence in Geiselmann's 1962 book, *The Meaning of Tradition*: 'Of Jesus Christ it is really true to say what a pope [Pius IX] once said of himself: I am tradition' (112). In *Christology: A Biblical, Historical, and Systematic Study of Jesus*, 2nd edn (Oxford: Oxford University Press, 2009), 334–57, I develop a Christology of presence; this Christology has been taken further by Cyril Orji, 'Does a Hermeneutical Clarification of "Presence" Advance O'Collins's Christology?', *New Blackfriars* 98 (2017), 653–75.

[36] *Montreal 1963*, 52; we return below to the problem attached to the language of 'content'.

[37] Ibid. 54; emphasis added.

[38] In *Christology*, I developed a Christology of Presence (334–57), but without using the term *Christus praesens*.

To apply the language of *Dei Verbum*, through the Holy Spirit, Christ provides 'everything that contributes to making the People of God live their life in holiness and grow in faith' (*DV* 8).

Both the Montreal report and *Dei Verbum* bring out the intimate connection between the presence of Christ and the action of the Spirit. While distinct, the missions of the Son and the Spirit are mutually interdependent. This brings us to the third item in the converging lines of agreement: *the invisible role of the Holy Spirit*, whose 'operation' transmits the 'living reality' that is 'the Christian tradition'.[39] While the whole people of God form the visible transmitters of Tradition, the transmission takes place primarily through the power of the Holy Spirit. Hence, as Congar insisted, it is ultimately the Spirit of Christ who maintains the integrity of the Tradition, and thus guarantees the Church's essential fidelity to the foundational experience of the divine self-communication in Christ.[40] *Dei Verbum* introduced what amounted to the same point: 'the Holy Spirit, through whom the living voice of the Gospel rings out in the Church and through her in the world, leads the believers into all truth, and makes the word of Christ dwell abundantly in them' (*DV* 8).

Fourth, among those who transmit tradition, do some enjoy an authoritative role, a magisterium that has the role of maintaining a needed unity (not uniformity) in teaching and interpreting the good news of Christ within changing contexts and new cultures? Here we come to a certain limit in the ecumenical convergence. The Montreal report largely leaves this question in the background. It contents itself with speaking about 'churches' and different 'confessional' traditions, sometimes simply naming differences between Anglicans, Baptists, Orthodox, Roman Catholics, and so on. In *Dei Verbum*, however, Vatican II, after reflecting on the role of the whole people of God as transmitters of tradition (*DV* 8), draws attention to the specific role of the bishops in officially interpreting tradition as well as Scripture (*DV* 10).

---

[39] *Montreal 1963*, 52.

[40] Congar, *Tradition and Traditions*, 338–46. Given his stress on the Holy Spirit's maintaining the integrity of tradition, it was no accident that, after his major work on tradition, Congar prepared another classic: *I Believe in the Holy Spirit*, trans. D. Smith, 3 vols (London: Geoffrey Chapman, 1983; French orig. 1980–3).

Fifth, I have noted (point two above) the total view of Tradition or *Traditum* which both *Dei Verbum* and the Montreal report proposed. The one *Traditum*, however, is expressed through many *tradita* or traditions. The Montreal report illustrated how this expression in different traditions applies in the spheres of liturgy, doctrine, mission, and life: 'Tradition taken in this sense is actualized in the preaching of the Word, in the administration of the sacraments and worship, in Christian teaching and theology, and in mission and witness to Christ by the lives of the members of the Church.'[41]

In this terminology, the specific traditions become 'expressions and manifestations in diverse historical forms of the one truth and reality which is Christ'.[42] Vatican II's decree on ecumenism, *Unitatis Redintegratio*, suggested similarly how the one *Traditum* gets expressed in the many *tradita*: 'this whole heritage (*patrimonium*) of spirituality and liturgy, of discipline and theology, in its various traditions belongs to the full catholicity and apostolicity of the Church' (*UR* 17).

Sixth, this actualizing of the one Tradition in the many traditions entails not only a rich diversity but also a recurrent challenge. Granted that we never find the Tradition 'neat' but always embedded in various traditions, do all of these traditions embody authentically the essential *Traditum*? The Montreal report put the issue this way: 'Do all traditions that claim to be Christian contain [*sic*] the Tradition? How can we distinguish between traditions embodying the true Tradition and merely human traditions? Where do we find the genuine Tradition, and where impoverished tradition or even distortion of tradition?'[43] Later the report repeats this distinction but in terms of being faithful or unfaithful: the one Tradition is 'expressed with *different degrees of fidelity* in various historically conditioned forms, namely the traditions'.[44] This involves the challenge of finding, when faced with particular, historical traditions, the 'right' interpretation of Scripture—that is to say, the interpretation 'guided by the Holy Spirit'.[45]

---

[41] *Montreal 63*, 52.   [42] Ibid.

[43] Ibid. This language of 'containing' is suitably qualified later: 'the content of the Tradition cannot be exactly defined, for the reality it transmits [Christ himself present in the life of the Church] can never be fully contained in propositional forms' (ibid. 58).

[44] Ibid. 55; emphasis added.   [45] Ibid. 53.

A year later, at the third session of Vatican II, Cardinal Albert Meyer of Chicago raised what was essentially the same issue during a debate on the text that would become *Dei Verbum*. He pointed to the 'limits' and 'defects' which show up repeatedly in the history of the Church and her traditions. He offered some examples: the long neglect of the doctrine of the resurrection, an exaggerated casuistry in moral theology, a non-liturgical piety, and the neglect of the Bible. He asked that the text under consideration should admit the existence of such defects and invoke the Scriptures as the norm that always helps the Church correct and perfect its life.[46] In fact, Cardinal Meyer's suggested addition was not adopted. But the final text of *Dei Verbum* did at least insist that the Scriptures should constantly 'rejuvenate' theology and the life of the Church (*DV* 24).

Dei Verbum did not address this question of discerning 'the Tradition within the traditions', but left the task of spelling out principles that should guide such discernment to other documents: for instance, the Constitution on the Sacred Liturgy (*Sacrosanctum Concilium*), the Decree on the Renewal of Religious Life (*Perfectae Caritatis*), and the Declaration on Religious Freedom (*Dignitatis Humanae*). The Decree on Ecumenism (*Unitatis Redintegratio*) clearly implied the need to discern and purify various traditions. It spoke of 'the Church called by Christ' to a 'constant reformation which she perpetually needs' (*UR* 6). Here it echoed what the Dogmatic Constitution on the Church (*Lumen Gentium*) said about the Church 'at once holy and always in need of purification' and following 'constantly' the way of 'penance and renewal' (*LG* 8).

Seventhly and finally, *Dei Verbum* alerted its readers to a central difficulty in using the inspired Scriptures towards discerning and reforming particular traditions. On the one hand, the whole Church and members of the magisterium should 'religiously listen to the Word of God' and 'proclaim it faithfully' (*DV* 1). The bishops are 'not above it [the Word]' but should serve it (*DV* 10). On the other hand, the same constitution alerted its readers to the difficulty of using the Scriptures as the only source of certainty in assenting to given truths—or to transpose matters into the precise point of our discussion—as the sole

---

[46] *Acta Synodalia Concilii Vaticani II*, III/III, 150–1.

means for establishing where the authentic tradition is to be found among the diverse traditions. Hinting at the *sola Scriptura* principle, *Dei Verbum* declared: 'the Church does not draw her certainty about all revealed matters *through the holy Scripture alone*' (*DV* 9; emphasis added).

A year before the Fourth World Conference on Faith and Order met in Montreal, Ernst Käsemann, who would attend the conference as an adviser, gave a lecture 'Thoughts on the Present Controversy about Scriptural Interpretation'. He understood *sola Scriptura* as meaning that the Church should be 'under' and not 'above' the Word of God:

> The relationship of the community and the Word of God is not reversible; there is no dialectical process by which the community created by the Word of God becomes at the same time for all practical purposes an authority set over the Word to interpret it, to administer it, to possess it. Naturally the community has always the task of interpreting the Word afresh, so that it can become audible at all times and in all places. In a certain sense it has also the task of administering it, inasmuch as it creates ways and means for the Word to make itself heard. But possess it—never. For the community remains the handmaid of the Word.[47]

Käsemann anticipated here the teaching of *Dei Verbum* about first hearing with reverence the Word of God before (interpreting it afresh and) proclaiming it with faith, or, in Käsemann's terms, letting the Word 'become audible at all times and in all places'. His vision of the community being 'under' and not 'above' the Word of God anticipated what *Dei Verbum* would say about the official teachers of the Church: 'the magisterium is not above the Word of God but is its minister [read 'handmaid']' (*DV* 10).[48]

The Montreal report recognized, nevertheless, a central difficulty that affects interpreting the Word of God and creating 'ways and means for the Word to make itself heard'. It admitted: 'loyalty to our confessional understanding of Holy Scripture produces both convergence and divergence in the interpretation of Scripture ... How can

---

[47] Käsemann, *New Testament Questions of Today*, 260–85, at 261–2.

[48] The ordination ceremony for bishops in the Latin rite illustrates vividly being a servant or handmaid of the Word of God: during the prayer of ordination, two deacons stand alongside the kneeling candidate and hold over his head the Book of the Gospels.

we overcome the situation in which we all read the Scripture in the light of our own tradition?'[49] Inherited traditions and other presuppositions cause Christians to create meaning, as well as discover it, when they read and interpret the Bible. Hence it does not seem either feasible or even possible to use the Scriptures as the *sole* criterion for sorting out defective and authentic traditions, so as to find the Tradition within the traditions. What other criteria might support the Scriptures in the task of discernment and interpretation? We will return to this issue in Chapter 6.

The aim of this chapter has been to draw on the Reformation controversy and two twentieth-century documents, the 1963 Montreal report of the Faith and Order Commission and the Constitution on Divine Revelation of the Second Vatican Council. The two texts suggest convergent lines of thinking and so provide a background towards discussing today the nature and role of tradition for Christians.

Major convergences, along with remaining differences of doctrine and emphasis, are set out very well in a joint statement published by American Lutherans and Roman Catholics, *Scripture and Tradition*.[50] This balanced and learned product of ecumenical dialogue does much to defuse the old arguments about Scripture and tradition and lends support to the narrative developed in this chapter.

Conclusion

This chapter took as its starting point James Mackey's *The Modern Theology of Tradition*, published in the same year as a work on tradition by Josef Rupert Geiselmann. Besides the attention Geiselmann paid to the teaching at Council of Trent and its aftermath, he set himself in his 1962 study to illustrate how at the beginning of Christianity God's revelation in Christ was handed down by tradition. As a cultural and social phenomenon, this Jewish–Christian tradition was a form, albeit the most perfect form, of a universal human reality: religious tradition. Hence Geiselmann, unlike Mackey and many others, was concerned to situate Christian tradition within a human context, tradition as studied by social scientists, especially cultural anthropologists like Mircea Eliade.[51]

In the more than five decades since Geiselmann's 1962 book appeared, further valuable studies of tradition have come from sociologists, cultural anthropologists, and other social scientists. But his intuition retains its value. When we examine Christian tradition, we need to reflect on tradition as a human reality and hear what social scientists say. Christian tradition may transcend but it does include a sociological and anthropological dimension. To this we turn in the next chapter.

---

[51] Geiselmann, *Die heilige Schrift und die Tradition*, 61–83; the 1966 English version of this book (see nn. 8 and 10 above) translated only the first part of the 1962 German original, omitting nearly two hundred pages on the Scripture/Tradition issue at Trent and beyond (84–282).

2

Tradition and Human Life

Some Sociological Views

As the study of society and patterns of human relationship, the discipline of sociology sheds light on social order and change. It promises to help us understand and interpret those networks, processes, and developments which shape human tradition, whether explicitly religious or otherwise. After presenting a theological convergence between the World Council of Churches' Faith and Order Commission and the Second Vatican Council on the nature and function of Christian tradition, we now examine insights into tradition coming from some specialists in sociology. This turn to sociology seeks 'inside' assistance towards constructing a theology of tradition, but does not aim to reduce religious tradition to a merely human affair.

Shils, Parsons, Martin, Berger, and Giddens

In 1981 Edward Shils (1910–95), a University of Chicago sociologist of world standing, published *Tradition*, a book that included a thought experiment to illustrate the pervasive influence of inherited tradition and past history in the present.

> If we could imagine a society in which each generation created all that it used, contemplated, enjoyed, and suffered, we would be imagining a society unlike any which has ever existed. It would be a society formed from a state of nature. It would literally be a society without a past to draw on and guide its actions in the present.[1]

[1] E. Shils, *Tradition* (London: Faber and Faber, 1981), 34.

In fact, tradition is so formative that all human beliefs and actions recall and embody some traditional elements received from past history. The inherited past is constantly and everywhere reflected in the present.

Shils did not ignore the ways in which individuals and whole generations could be strikingly creative. He pointed to the 'unprecedented degrees' of change in Western societies, which, 'more than the societies a century or two centuries ago', have achieved 'innovations in economic, social, and political organization and in technology and scientific knowledge'. But Shils rejected as 'hyperbole' the notion 'that our societies have been totally transformed in the past century'. 'They have certainly changed', he agreed, 'but they have also changed along [traditional] lines laid down by their previous state, and certain features have not changed as much as others'. 'Many of the beliefs and patterns of action of any Western society a century ago still exist and are important.' Shils cited 'modes of political life, the organization of universities, types of religious institutions, beliefs, and ritual, and the legal system'.[2] He had no difficulty in demonstrating that, no matter how human beings modify inherited beliefs and change traditional patterns of action, the new always incorporates something of the past.[3]

All of this made Shils regret 'the blindness of social sciences to tradition'. 'Tradition', he reflected, 'is a dimension of social structure which is lost or hidden by the a-temporal conceptions which now prevail in the social sciences'.[4] He was thinking of sociologists who preferred such expressions as 'social forces'.[5]

When we recall other leaders in the social sciences, we might start with Shils's contemporary, the Harvard University sociologist Talcott Parsons (1902–79). His widely read *The Social System*[6] showed some interest in the ways that authoritative traditionalism resists modernity. Yet he neither embraced the more 'neutral' stance embodied in the term adopted by Shils, 'traditionality',[7] nor attempted any lengthy account of tradition as such.

---

[2] Ibid. 37.   [3] Ibid. 34–62.   [4] Ibid. 7.   [5] Ibid. 8–9.
[6] (London: Routledge & Kegan Paul, 1970).
[7] On 'traditionality' as 'an intrinsic value', see Shils, *Tradition*, 328–30.

A year before Shils published *Tradition*, there appeared a study of the relationship between sociology and theology. It emerged from meetings held in England by a group that included the prominent sociologist of religion David Martin (b. 1929). This joint study set out ways in which sociology can contribute to theology, but had nothing to say about sociology's possible contribution towards evaluating tradition, religious or otherwise.[8] Subsequently a 1997 work by Martin, despite its title (*Reflections on Sociology and Theology*), added nothing towards appreciating sociologically the place of tradition in religion.[9]

Yet a few of Shils's younger contemporaries did lift up the theme of 'tradition' for examination. Peter Berger (1929–2017), who taught at Boston University, Rutgers University, and elsewhere, proved a notable and widely read example.[10] He wrote of 'the embodiment of human experiences in traditions and institutions' as 'a general feature of human existence'.[11] Experience—and, in particular, religious experience—motivates the emergence of traditions: 'religious experience . . . comes to be embodied in traditions, which mediate it to those who have not had it themselves, and which institutionalize it for them as well as for those who have had it'.[12] Berger also endorsed the importance of collective memory: 'every tradition is a collective memory'. In his view, 'religious tradition is a collective memory of those moments in which the reality of another world broke into the paramount reality of everyday life'.[13] In the appendix I will examine the value of interpreting Christian tradition as a collective memory.

---

[8] D. Martin, J. O. Mills, and W. S. F. Pickering (eds), *Sociology and Theology: Alliance and Conflict* (Brighton: Harvester Press, 1980).

[9] D. Martin, *Reflections on Sociology and Theology* (Oxford: Clarendon Press, 1997).

[10] See P. L. Berger, *The Heretical Imperative: Contemporary Possibilities of Religious Affirmation* (London: Collins, 1980); and *The Sacred Canopy: Elements of a Sociological Theory of Religion* (Garden City, NY: Doubleday, 1967).

[11] Berger, *Heretical Imperative*, 46. He developed this theme in P. L. Berger and T. Luckmann, *The Social Construction of Reality: A Treatise on the Sociology of Knowledge* (Garden City, NY: Doubleday, 1967), 67–72, 116–18.

[12] Berger, *The Heretical Imperative*, 46.

[13] Ibid. 49. In his entry 'Tradition', in Lindsay Jones (ed.), *Encyclopedia of Religion*, xiii (Detroit: Thomson Gale, 2005), 9267–81, at 9268, Paul Valliere writes of 'the critical importance of memory in religious traditions'. Shils agrees that memory is crucial for understanding tradition: see *Tradition*, 50–3, 80–1, 92–4, 166–7.

But I must agree that, while Berger resonated in theology, it was more for his insights into the signs of transcendence than for his reflections on tradition and, specifically, on tradition as collective memory.[14]

In the 1990s the theme of tradition entered a joint study by Ulrich Beck, Anthony Giddens, and Scott Lash: *Reflexive Modernization: Politics, Tradition and Aesthetics in the Modern Social Order*.[15] In other works Giddens (b. 1938),[16] through a scheme of traditional (pre-modern) culture contrasted with 'post-traditional' (modern) culture, has presented the picture of developed modernity having 'detraditionalized' cultures and spelt the death of many traditional ways. Two worlds collided and frequently age-old traditions could not survive the encounter with modernity. Where in pre-modern societies tradition used to dictate choices, 'modern' human beings show themselves less concerned with the precedents they have inherited from earlier generations, and can often make more 'informed', 'reflexive' choices than their ancestors. Below we will attend to a widely read study by Giddens, *Runaway World: How Globalisation is Reshaping Our Lives*.[17]

Here it is worth noting how the Second Vatican Council's Constitution on the Church in the Modern World, *Gaudium et Spes* (promulgated 7 December 1965), briefly anticipated reflections coming from Giddens. After describing the vast changes that urbanization, globalized communication, and mass migration were bringing, *Gaudium et Spes* remarked: 'peoples, particularly those committed to older traditions, are experiencing a movement towards a more mature and more

---

[14] See the use made of Berger in W. Pannenberg's magisterial work, *Anthropology in Theological Perspective*, trans. M. J. O'Connell (Edinburgh: T. & T. Clark, 2004; German orig. 1985). Rather than elucidate tradition, Pannenberg spends many pages on the closely related theme of culture (ibid. 315–484), a discussion which could often be transposed in terms of tradition. Take e.g. what he quotes from Arnold Gehlen: 'all cultures . . . have at their base systems of stereotyped and stable habits' (ibid. 403). Here we might equivalently speak of 'systems of stable traditions'; traditions play a supporting role in all areas of culture.

[15] (Stanford, CA: Stanford University Press, 1994); see also P. Boyer, *Tradition as Truth and Communication: A Cognitive Description of Traditional Discourse* (Cambridge: Cambridge University Press, 1990).

[16] See e.g. A. Giddens, *Modernity and Self-identity: Self and Society in the Late Modern Age* (Cambridge: Polity, 1991).

[17] (London: Profile, 2002).

personal exercise of freedom' (*GS* 6). Later the constitution also briefly anticipated Giddens's picture of modernity 'detraditionalizing' cultures when it asked: 'How is the dynamism and expansion of the new culture to be supported without a living loyalty to inherited traditions being lost?' (*GS* 56).[18]

We can put this dilemma concretely in terms, for instance, of Africa's disappearing cultures. As modernity continues to creep in, traditional African tribes remain caught between the allure of modern life and a desire to save their traditions. Should they hold on to the past or allow themselves to be assimilated by the forces of modernity?

When John Thiel came to write *Senses of Tradition: Continuity and Development in Catholic Faith*, he did not quote from Shils, Berger, Giddens, or any other sociologists when he spoke in passing of the 'sociological perspectives that have served this study'.[19] Let us continue to see what such perspectives might look like, if we take up first some perspectives from Shils and Berger, and then turn to those of Giddens.

The Past in the Present

Sadly the valuable study by Shils on tradition seems to have been widely ignored by theologians writing on tradition, whether they

---

[18] In two other documents (the Constitution on the Sacred Liturgy and the Decree on the Church's Missionary Activity), the Second Vatican Council showed interest in human traditions: 'the traditions of individual peoples' (*SC* 37–40) and, specifically, marriage, funeral, and musical traditions (*SC* 77, 81, 112, 119); and then, more generally, 'the traditions' of people—especially, 'local traditions' (*AG* 22).

[19] (New York: Oxford University Press, 2000), 40. No sociologists are named when Thiel writes of 'a sociological point of view in which common readings and understandings achieve an authority which is largely uncontested' (ibid. 38). In an endnote, the critical social theory of Jürgen Habermas is fleetingly noted, along with the work of an American sociologist, John Coleman (ibid. 244–5). When Thiel turns to non-theological partners in his discussion, he repeatedly introduces such philosophers as Donald Davidson, Hans-Georg Gadamer, Willard Quine, Paul Ricoeur, and Wilfrid Sellars. Here he resembles Peter Lengsfeld who brings in philosophical (but not sociological) reflections (citing Gadamer, Martin Heidegger, Josef Pieper, and other philosophers) when examining tradition: 'Tradition innerhalb der konstitutiven Zeit der Offenbarung', in J. Feiner and M. Löhrer (eds), *Mysterium Salutis*, i (Einsiedeln: Benziger Verlag, 1965), 239–88, at 240–51.

composed books, book chapters, articles, or dictionary entries. Günther Gassmann, for instance, has nothing to say about Shils or any other sociologist (or, for that matter, any cultural anthropologist) in his entry on 'Tradition'.[20] Hermann Josef Pottmeyer recognizes how 'tradition is a constitutive element of human culture'. He begins his entry on 'Tradition' by reflecting on the 'phenomenon of human culture', but does not cite Shils or other social scientists.[21] Paul Valliere in an entry on 'Tradition' does, however, highlight the contribution of Shils and his 'excellent introduction to the concept of tradition'.[22]

What lasting value is found in the approach to tradition developed by Shils? It is, he states, as 'the past in the present' that tradition makes its essential 'difference' in 'human life'.[23] Let me single out four points that should be retrieved.

First, Shils takes a *global view* of this persistence of the past: it is tradition which embodies everything that individuals inherit when born into this world.[24] This 'past in the present' involves all manner of institutions (e.g. families, schools, parliaments, and churches); enduring practices, beliefs, and ideals of various societies; a wealth of human knowledge already acquired by scientific observation[25] and

[20] In E. Fahlbusch et al. (eds), *The Encyclopedia of Christianity*, trans. G. W. Bromiley, v (Grand Rapids, MI: Eerdmans, 2008), 517–19.

[21] In R. Latourelle and R. Fisichella (eds), *Dictionary of Fundamental Theology* (New York: Crossroad, 1994), 119–26, at 119–21.

[22] In *Encyclopedia of Religion*, xiii, 9280.   [23] Shils, *Tradition*, vii.

[24] Ibid. 54. The global or total view of tradition endorsed by the 1963 report of the Faith and Order Commission and Vatican II in 1965 (see the previous chapter) simply expresses a general feature of tradition, religious or otherwise.

[25] On tradition in science, see Shils, *Tradition*, 100–20. Shils offers fascinating pages on 'the tradition of skill' and 'the tradition of invention' (ibid. 93–9). He points out how 'innovation in technology' has become 'a pervasive tradition' in modern times (ibid. 88). 'Unthinking adherents of *scientism* [the belief that science is the only source of genuine knowledge]' may proclaim an 'antithesis between tradition and science', but even a 'scientific genius cannot live without tradition'. As Shils adds, 'untutored genius in science is rendered utterly improbable because genius requires for its capacities to become effective that it be inserted into a tradition and even into a community . . . which embodies that tradition in its activities' (ibid. 119; emphasis added). See also M. Oakeshott, *Rationalism in Politics and Other Essays* (London: Methuen, 1962), 123.

through other forms of research;[26] material objects like existing build-ings (e.g. houses of parliament and cathedrals) that are preserved and not torn down; images received from the past like paintings, statues, flags, crucifixes, Christmas cribs, and Eastern icons; innumerable books (including copies of the Bible and other religious texts), manu-scripts, and tapes housed in libraries, archives, churches, and monas-teries; the language(s)[27] and literature of a nation or country (including their written constitutions and stories of founding figures and events); all kinds of secular and sacred beliefs, values, modes of acting, and past judgements that feed into the common law tradition; and much else besides.

Shils develops his total view of tradition in two chapters: 'the endurance of past objects' and 'the endurance of past practices'.[28] He points out that 'material objects have a self-maintaining power which is inherent in their material nature'. He takes cities as an example. It is 'often economically [and one could also say aesthetic-ally] advantageous to maintain older buildings'. Many buildings, 'built long before the birth of those now living, mark the cities of the earth. The fame of a city depends on having such buildings.'[29] As someone who lives in a nineteenth-century house, often photo-graphed by passing tourists, I warmly concur with Shils's view of past tradition and history being embodied in buildings we inherit and inhabit.

Shils cites too traditional objects housed in buildings: 'old furniture and old table silver are like old buildings. They are used and they are

---

[26] Giddens writes similarly: 'we shouldn't accept the Enlightenment idea that the world should rid itself of tradition altogether. Traditions are needed and will always persist, because they give continuity and form to life. Take academic life, as an example. Everyone in the academic world works within tradition' (*Runaway World*, 44–5).

[27] Because of immediate, sensory stimulation, we may say 'it's raining'. Doing so, however, involves shared, traditional language that we have inherited.

[28] Shils, *Tradition*, 63–161 and 162–94.

[29] Ibid. 63. Shils draws particular attention to two classes of old buildings: 'a large proportion of the buildings surviving for three or more centuries in most civilizations are buildings which were used for religious worship or for imperial or royal residence, or were otherwise connected with divine things or with earthly power and majesty' (ibid. 68).

appreciated for their utility, their beauty, and their age.'[30] Yet, even more, contemporary people treasure works of art: 'the modern world which in many respects so resolutely set itself against traditional beliefs and traditional patterns of conduct has devoted relatively large resources to the assembly, protection, and exhibition of old works of art and old books in manuscript and printed form'.[31]

Second, new members of society may come to hold that their personal flourishing requires being liberated from 'the dead hand of the past', those inherited norms, ideals, and modes of thinking which have been handed on to them. They may not want to live according to particular traditions they have received. But initially tradition teaches them all the 'givens' with which they begin to live and *identify themselves*. They will learn for themselves, but so much of the knowledge they enjoy and act upon will remain knowledge they have received from representatives of their tradition rather than knowledge they have been able to acquire or at least check for themselves. No individuals, even the most intellectually gifted, could ever hope to master the whole of the tradition that has been passed on to them.

Whatever stance individuals take towards tradition, the inherited past inevitably shapes ways in which they identify themselves. As Shils remarks, a sense of their 'own identity is partly a present perception' of their past.[32] He recognizes how this past includes images of what 'ancestors did, were, and believed', images that affect present conduct.[33] Living now in Australia, I am constantly confronted with such self-identifying images that have their impact on Aboriginal peoples and on the wider population. The annual celebration of Anzac Day (25 April), centred on the huge Shrine of Remembrance that dominates the southern approach to Melbourne, for instance, recalls the landing of Australian and other troops at Gallipoli (Turkey) in 1915 and presents their heroic deeds as worthy of veneration and emulation.

[30] Ibid. 71.   [31] Ibid. 74.

[32] Ibid. 50. Elsewhere Shils writes of receiving and responding: people 'are what they are because they have been formed by the traditions they have received and by the contemporary circumstances to which they have responded' (ibid. 54).

[33] Ibid. 53.

With Anzac Day, we reach the way in which tradition affects the self-identity not only of individuals but also of societies. Traditions, including those traditions that result from scientific enquiry, come together to organize and manage society. Tradition enables a society to cohere, identify itself, and continue. Both collectively and individually, tradition always contributes in one way or another to a sense of self-identity and to social cohesion.

The traditions of a nation, group, and religious body may be transmitted very consciously: for instance, in ceremonies through which migrants receive the citizenship of their host country or through which Christians are baptized and commit themselves to observe the basic elements of existing tradition. Or else traditions are transmitted unconsciously: for instance, through language, a supreme product of human tradition, which enshrines the wisdom of the ages.

Third, *the agents for preserving and handing on* tradition—Shils calls them 'the bearers of tradition'[34]—may be official, such as the leaders of long-enduring institutions and teachers in such institutions. But they can also be painters, freelance writers, sculptors, and composers of hymns. Think of Rembrandt and his sense of transmitting the religious tradition of Judaism and Christianity. His 1661 self-portrait showed him as the apostle Paul. He also associated the present with the past—in this case with medieval, mendicant religious—by painting his son as a Franciscan monk.

Shils distinguishes the 'learned' from the 'ordinary believers' as bearers of religious tradition. In both cases, practice is essential; tradition is sustained by its 'recurrent reaffirmation'.[35]

Few authors evoke so skilfully and affectionately the astounding monuments of Christian tradition as does Simon Jenkins.[36] When presenting his 1,000 'best' examples of churches in England, he draws overwhelmingly from the roughly 8,000 Anglo-Saxon, Norman, and Gothic pre-Reformation churches that have survived. Those who want to know what the traditional faith of English Catholicism from the eleventh to the sixteenth centuries looked like could well be guided by Jenkins and look at the testimonies left in stone, wood, and glass.

---

[34] Ibid. 262; see 96–7.   [35] Ibid. 95–6.

[36] S. Jenkins, *England's Thousand Best Churches* (London: Penguin, 1999).

In these permanent ways, 'ordinary' medieval believers continue to transmit to us their tradition of faith.

Fourth, studying tradition inevitably throws up two issues that prove vital towards understanding and *discerning tradition*: (a) the lasting truth and authority of tradition, and (b) change in tradition. What gives normative value to some inherited beliefs and practices? What prompts changes in tradition and what might justify those changes? Shils dedicates many pages to factors that change traditions.[37] More briefly but with enviable clarity, he illustrates ways in which historical research can have its impact on inherited traditions.[38]

In a later chapter we will take up these questions and explore what is required in discerning, changing, abolishing, and reinstating traditions. This challenge includes but goes well beyond a much studied theme: development of doctrine.

Runaway Challenges to Tradition

In his Reith Lectures, published as *Runaway World: How Globalisation is Reshaping Our Lives*, Giddens uses the subtitle of his book to name one huge force in our modern world that more and more affects local cultures and traditions. *Globalization* in communications, trade, investments, movements of people, dissemination of knowledge, and other forms continues to reshape societies around the world and, in many cases, to spell the death of inherited traditions. Interdependence in the world's economy has repeatedly brought an 'outsourcing' that ends local industries and traditions linked to them, as well as disrupting the traditional village life of developing countries.

Globalization involves unprecedented advances in communication. Through the internet and mobile phones, people from the ends of the earth can be instantly connected. Breaking news, transmitted at once from a distant country, may assume world significance. Hundreds of millions of human beings now watch the Olympic Games and World Cup finals of soccer. On 6 September 1997, a global audience of around 2.5 billion people followed on television the funeral of Princess Diana at Westminster Abbey; many of them joined in reciting the

---

[37] Shils, *Tradition*, 213–61.   [38] Ibid. 54–62.

(traditional) Lord's Prayer when invited to do so by the presiding celebrant, the then Archbishop of Canterbury, George Carey. On 8 April 2005, up to three billion people around the globe watched the televised funeral (in St Peter's Square) of St John Paul II (pope 1978–2005) or followed it on radio.

Global communication can also involve the sidelining of local cultures and the loss of the traditional perspectives of specific societies. How far will the worldwide media facilitate the decline of particular cultures and traditions?

Giddens has also examined extensively two other areas in which the runaway world has radically impacted on traditional society. Sweeping changes in life-style are now permitted by shifts in law and public opinion: for instance, on same-sex marriage and the 'right' to suicide. It is obvious that *traditional boundaries controlling human choices and behaviour have been extended*. I write this page the day after my sister-in-law found that the taxi she took in Melbourne was driven by an Ethiopian who is married to a Cambodian. The driver mentioned that in a few days' time he and his wife would fly to Rome to visit his sister; she is married to an Italian and has six children. Well beyond the possibilities envisaged by the traditions into which they were born, people, like the Ethiopian taxi driver and his sister, can exercise choices and 'actualize themselves' in unprecedented ways.

Giddens notes how this self-actualization can also bring heightened *uncertainty*.[39] Pre-modern, traditional society enjoyed fewer choices but normally supported people in reassuring ways. The runaway world has now moved millions from village and rural life to a frequently lonely and fearful existence in mega-cities. Here we should not forget how wars, often aided and abetted by developed countries, have made over sixty million people displaced within their own nation, gathered abroad in refugee camps, or hopelessly trying to cross national frontiers as asylum seekers. The wars of the twenty-first century have continued to wreck traditional ways of life.

Giddens does not ignore the aggressive plundering of nature which threatens the world, its cultures, and traditions through *climate change,*

---

[39] On risk-taking and risk-management, see Giddens, *Runaway World*, 20–35.

deforestation, and *further destruction of natural resources.*[40] As I write this page, I have just read a report from the World Health Organization about deaths caused by air pollution: such pollution kills more than a million Chinese each year. In a remarkable exchange of letters with Cardinal Carlo Maria Martini about the future of our race and planet, Umberto Eco listed twenty years ago some ecological and other major threats:

> the uncontrolled and uncontrollable proliferation of nuclear waste; acid rain; the disappearing Amazon; the hole in the ozone; the migrating, disinherited masses knocking, often with violence, at the doors of prosperity; the hunger of entire continents; new, incurable pestilence; the selfish destruction of the soil; global warming; meltdown glaciers; the construction of our own clones through genetic engineering.[41]

Far from being eliminated, many of these threats have become more acute.

This chapter has taken inspiration from Berger, Giddens, and, especially, Shils to suggest what sociologists might contribute to Christian thinking about tradition and its functions for their (and other) religious faiths: for instance, by promoting collective consciousness and various beliefs and practices that serve to support the community's life. The sociologists have also made permanence and change significant areas of enquiry. As Shils remarked, in general, religion may be 'thought to be the stronghold of traditionality', but 'innovation' occurs.[42] This certainly holds true of the world's oldest and largest religious institution, the Roman Catholic Church. Traditional beliefs (e.g. the ancient creeds), rituals (e.g. the seven sacraments), functionaries (e.g. bishops), patterns of behaviour, and innumerable particular traditions continue to shape its daily life around the world. Yet great innovations have been introduced: for instance, by the Second Vatican Council (1962–5). We turn next to reflect on

---

[40] A. Giddens, *The Politics of Climate Change* (Cambridge: Polity, 2009); see also Pope Francis, *Laudato Si'* (Vatican City: Libreria Editrice Vaticana, 2015), an encyclical letter on ecology and climate change.

[41] U. Eco and C. M. Martini, *Belief or Non-Belief: A Confrontation* (New York: Arcade Publishing, 2000), 21.

[42] Shils, *Tradition*, 27–8.

tradition, in its permanence and innovation, as it affects the Catholic Church and wider Christianity. But, before doing so, let us raise the question: Has sociology appeared in theological discussions of tradition?

Theologies of Tradition and Sociology

Numerous theologians have engaged with the social sciences and, specifically, with sociology. One can cite, for instance, John Milbank, Edward Schillebeeckx, and Graham Ward. But they have not, or at least have not explicitly, investigated Christian *tradition* with the help of sociologists. They have brought sociology into dialogue with theology in general rather than the theology of tradition in particular.[43] Ward engages with leading German sociologists, has a good deal to say about culture, but like Schillebeeckx does not explicitly introduce the topic of tradition. Milbank knows the modern social sciences, but has argued that theologians do not need them, since Christian theology itself is already an alternative social science.[44]

Have such feminist theologians as Elizabeth Johnson engaged directly with tradition and done so in the light of the social sciences? Her classic *She Who Is: The Mystery of God in Feminist Theological Discourse*, while including some brief remarks on 'revelation', has nothing at all on 'tradition'.[45] Her admirable *Truly Our Sister: A Theology of Mary in the Communion of Saints* lists nothing in the index on either 'revelation' or 'tradition'.[46] *In Memory of Her: A Feminist Reconstruction of Christian Origins* by Elisabeth Schüssler Fiorenza remains a landmark volume in feminist theology.[47] But, despite the very close connection between

---

[43] See J. Milbank, *Theology and Social Theory: Beyond Secular Reason* (Oxford: Blackwell, 2006); G. Ward, *Theology and Contemporary Theology*, 2nd edn (Basingstoke: Macmillan, 2000); *Christ: the Christian Experience in the Modern World, Collected Works of Edward Schillebeeckx*, vii (London: Bloomsbury, 2014) engages substantially with sociologists of the Frankfurt School, but has nothing to say explicitly about tradition.

[44] Milbank, *Theology and Social Theory*, 245–6, 389, and the whole of Ch. 12 ('The Other City: Theology as Social Science').

[45] (New York: Crossroad, 1992).   [46] (New York: Continuum, 2004).

[47] (London: SCM Press, 1983).

memory and tradition (see the appendix), she does not reflect on tradition as such, or at least does not do so explicitly.

A recent feminist exploration of the Eucharist, without introducing anything from the social sciences engages with some sacramental traditions. But it does not explicitly treat Christian tradition as such.[48]

One might have expected liberation theologians to have taken up 'tradition' explicitly and done so in the light of modern social sciences. But a standard study like A. T. Hennelly's *Liberation Theology: A Documentary History* reports nothing about discussions or debates concerned with tradition.[49] A significant work in liberation theology, Juan Luis Segundo's *Faith and Ideologies*, however, includes a good deal on tradition, especially Latin American traditions, and does so in the light of some sociological sources, notably Karl Marx.[50] But Gustavo Gutiérrez, generally considered the founder of liberation theology, remains quite silent about tradition in *A Theology of Liberation: History, Politics and Salvation*.[51] Trawling through classical liberation theologians like Leonardo Boff, one finds a certain alliance with social scientists. The social sciences help theologians to uncover the causes of oppression.[52] The liberation theologians re-read Christian history from the underside of the suffering poor, but have generally remained uninterested in probing the fundamental nature and function of Christian tradition, let alone doing so in dialogue with the social sciences. Even Segundo has the largely limited aim of examining some Latin American traditions and not tradition as such. A more recent work on liberation theology draws on the social sciences but includes nothing on 'tradition'.[53]

To conclude. Only a few theologians (see the bibliography) in recent years have directly examined aspects of Christian tradition.

---

[48] A. Elvey et al. (eds), *Reinterpreting the Eucharist: Explorations in Feminist Theology and Ethics* (Sheffield: Equinox, 2013).

[49] (Maryknoll, NY: Orbis Books, 1990).

[50] (Maryknoll, NY: Orbis Books, 1984), 305–40.

[51] (Maryknoll, NY: Orbis Books, 1973).

[52] See e.g. L. Boff, *Liberating Grace* (Maryknoll, NY: Orbis Books, 1979), and *Jesus Christ Liberator: A Critical Christology for Our Times* (Maryknoll, NY: Orbis Books, 1981).

[53] I. Petrella (ed.), *Latin American Liberation Theology: The Next Generation* (Maryknoll, NY: Orbis Books, 2005).

But they have uniformly failed to appropriate helpful insights they might have gained from Berger, Giddens, Shils, and other sociologists. Yet, when we examine the role of tradition, we should also reflect on tradition as a human reality and what the social scientists and, specifically, the sociologists, have to say. Admittedly, for years some theologians have used the social sciences to illuminate Christian theology in general. However, in the rare cases of contemporary theologians who have explored themes concerned explicitly with Christian tradition, I have looked in vain for any dialogue with sociologists.

3

Revelation, Tradition, and Culture

The receiving and handing on (*paradōsis*) of the Gospel feature in the first Christian documents. Paul reminds the Corinthians of an early creed that he transmitted to them: 'I handed on [*paredōka*] to you as of first importance what I in turn had received: that Christ died for our sins in accordance with the Scriptures, and that he was buried, and that he has been raised on the third day in accordance with the Scriptures, and that he appeared to Cephas, then to the Twelve' (1 Cor. 15: 3–5). To emphasize the credibility of this tradition, the apostle adds to the list of Easter witnesses two individuals (James and himself) and two groups (a gathering of more than 500 Christian faithful and 'all the apostles') (1 Cor. 15: 6–8).[1]

The author of the Letter of Jude explains his reason for writing this letter: 'I find it necessary to write and appeal to you to contend for the faith that was once and for all handed on [*paradotheisē*]' (Jude 3). A late New Testament text speaks briefly of 'the holy commandment that has been handed on [*paradotheisēs*]' (2 Pet. 2: 21).

Those to whom the Easter message, or 'the faith', or 'the holy commandment' has been handed on are expected to 'contend' for it and 'guard' it. Timothy is to 'guard what has been entrusted [*parathēkē*]' to him (1 Tim. 6: 20). Guarding the *parathēkē* becomes a theme at the opening of another letter (2 Tim. 1: 12, 14). Timothy is to 'entrust [*parathou*] to faithful people' what he has heard from Paul; they will 'teach others as well' (2 Tim. 2: 2).[2]

---

[1] On these verses from 1 Corinthians, see J. A. Fitzmyer, *First Corinthians* (New Haven, CT: Yale University Press, 2008), and A. C. Thiselton, *The First Epistle to the Corinthians* (Grand Rapids, MI: Eerdmans, 2000).

[2] On these verses from 1 and 2 Timothy, see L. T. Johnson, *The First and Second Letters to Timothy* (New York: Doubleday, 2001).

Signifying 'property that has been entrusted to another', *parathēkē* was used in an extended sense to mean all that God revealed through Christ for human salvation and was considered a treasure entrusted to the Church to be preserved and handed on faithfully to all people until the end of time. In other words, the *parathēkē* was understood to stand for the object of the Christian tradition (*paradōsis*), the heart of that which was handed on and aroused (and supported) faith. Since the Vulgate (Latin) translation of the New Testament used *depositum* to translate *parathēkē*, this object of Christian transmission came to be called 'the deposit of faith'. The Second Vatican Council spoke four times of 'the deposit of faith' (*LG* 25; *UR* 6; *DV* 10; *GS* 62), but also called it 'the sacred deposit' (*DV* 10), 'the deposit of the word of God' (*GS* 33), 'the deposit of Revelation' (*LG* 25) and 'the treasure of Revelation' (*DV* 26). How might we link this language of tradition as process (*paradōsis*) and object (*parathēkē*) with divine revelation, on the one hand, and with the writing of inspired Scripture, on the other?

Revelation Primarily and Secondarily

The reception of the divine self-revelation by human beings, beginning with half-glimpsed figures like Abraham and Sarah in the patriarchal period, determined the rise of Jewish–Christian religious tradition and then, through the gift of biblical inspiration, the composition of the Holy Scriptures. The experience of God's self-disclosure came 'to be embodied in traditions', which institutionalized those experiences and handed on the memory of them.[3] Thus the experience of divine self-revelation at the Last Supper and in the crucifixion and resurrection of Jesus was passed on and perpetuated when the Eucharist was celebrated. The Eucharist became an apostolic tradition recorded under biblical inspiration, first in 1 Corinthians 11: 23–6, and then in Mark 14: 22–6, Matthew 26: 26–30, and Luke 22: 14–23. The practice of the Eucharistic tradition, as 'the past in the present'[4] and tradition par excellence, made (and makes) an essential difference to the life of

---

[3] P. L. Berger, *The Heretical Imperative: Contemporary Possibilities of Religious Affirmation* (London: Collins, 1980), 46, 49.

[4] E. Shils, *Tradition* (London: Faber and Faber, 1981), vii.

Christians.[5] In Paul's words, the Eucharistic celebration means 'announcing the death of the [risen] Lord until he comes' (1 Cor. 15: 26). How should we describe in more detail revelation, the overarching reality that shapes tradition and Scripture?

Niels Gregersen offers a richly trinitarian description of divine revelation: 'The logic of revelation is inherently relational, insofar as a revelation is a revelation *of* something or somebody (God the Father) to somebody (human apprehenders of the revelation) *in and through* a medium of revelation (the Incarnate One) *by* a relational power (the Holy Spirit).'[6] This is to understand revelation as being primarily an interpersonal event: the tripersonal God being disclosed to human beings and triggering their faith. To this we need to add (and explain) the secondary, propositional meaning of revelation, as well as the past, present, and future reality of revelation.

Primarily, revelation meant the self-disclosure of God who is Truth itself (upper case and in the singular), a redemptive self-manifestation of God who called and empowered human beings (like Abraham, Sarah, and the disciples of Jesus) to accept a new, personal relationship of faith. After experiencing the presence of God, they could, *secondarily*, express this experience in true propositions and eventually

[5] See B. D. Spinks, *Do This in Remembrance of Me: The Eucharist from the Early Church to the Present Day* (London: SCM Press, 2013).

[6] N. H. Gregersen, 'The Extended Body of Christ: Three Dimensions of Deep Incarnation', in N. H. Gregersen (ed.), *Incarnation: On the Scope and Depth of Christology* (Minneapolis: Fortress Press, 2015), 225–51, at 238; emphasis original. For a full account of revelation, see G. O'Collins, *Revelation: Towards a Christian Interpretation of God's Self-revelation in Jesus Christ* (Oxford: Oxford University Press, 2016). In a review of this book (*Theology* 121 (2018), 68–70), Mark Ord argues that my distinction between revelation as primarily relational and secondarily propositional implies 'a dichotomy between the relational and the cognitive'. The *Oxford Dictionary of English* (3rd edn, 2009) defines 'dichotomy' as 'a division or contrast between two things that are or are represented as being opposed or entirely different'. My distinction between the primary and secondary meaning of revelation is a distinction, and certainly not a division or contrast between revelation as relational and revelation as propositional, as if they were opposed or entirely different. 'Dichotomy' seriously misrepresents my distinction—also expressed as 'knowledge *of God*' (emphasis on the relational) and 'knowledge *about* God' (emphasis on the cognitive) (*Revelation*, 13). Ord wanted 'more explicit Trinitarian reflection on revelation'. Is he happy with the quotation from Gregersen?

embody it in written, doctrinal traditions.[7] The first Christians summed up and interpreted their personal experience of Jesus crucified and risen from the dead through propositions expressed by four verbs: 'died', 'was buried', 'has been raised', and 'appeared' (1 Cor. 15: 3–5). They experienced his death and came to understand it as a death 'for our sins in accordance with the Scriptures'. Many of Jesus' first followers experienced him gloriously alive after his death and burial, and expressed this as resurrection 'on the third day in accordance with the Scriptures'. An early tradition, in the form of a creed, handed on these revealed truths (plural and in lower case) about the crucifixion and resurrection of Jesus. Divine revelation came primarily as a person and secondarily as a set of propositions.

Hence revelation was the experienced revelation of Someone, the Incarnate Son of God, who is the Truth (John 14: 6). It was then embodied in ceremonies (e.g. baptism and the Eucharist) and in the narratives and teachings of the inspired Scriptures. It would also be expressed in other traditions that are handed on: for instance, sacred art (e.g. early icons and musical compositions). In their turn, these traditional expressions of previous revelatory encounters with God could trigger fresh experiences of God. Thus tradition may prompt new events of personal divine self-disclosure.

Like the 1963 Faith and Order report from Montreal, Vatican II in 1965, as we saw in Chapter 1, firstly made it abundantly clear that revelation means primarily God's self-revelation (*DV* 1–4). *Dei Verbum* then moved to say: 'God graciously arranged that *the things he had revealed* for the salvation of all nations should remain in their entirely forever, and be transmitted to all generations' (*DV* 7; emphasis added). Since it deals with the transmission (or tradition) of revelation, that same, second chapter naturally speaks of 'all revealed things' (*DV* 9), and proceeds to use a classical term for the complete revelation communicated through Christ and his apostles: 'all that it [the magisterium of the bishops] proposes for belief as being divinely revealed is drawn from this one *deposit of faith*' (*DV* 10; emphasis added).

[7] Here I speak of the sequence for the initial recipients of significant revelation. But over the centuries many people have obviously come to know the doctrines and traditions before any personal experience 'kicked in'.

At the end, *Dei Verbum* introduces an equivalent, albeit happier, term when it speaks of 'the *treasure of Revelation* entrusted to the Church', which is to be faithfully preserved and proclaimed (*DV* 26; emphasis added). Although the 'deposit of faith' can claim its source in New Testament letters, 'deposit' suggests too easily a bank deposit or an alluvial deposit. It suffers from similar problems in other languages. At an Italian railway station, the *deposito* is the hall where you can leave or 'deposit' your luggage. When a railway carriage is moved '*in deposito*', it is being shifted to the yards. This is the language of things which we can act upon—by depositing or withdrawing money, exca-vating the earth, leaving luggage, or taking a carriage off the main tracks. 'Treasure' is also a thing but, in various languages, it carries warmly positive overtones of someone or even somebody who acts powerfully upon us. It can remind us of Jesus' parable about 'the treasure hidden in a field' to be acquired at all costs (Matt. 13: 44), and of his invitation to store up treasure in heaven: 'where your treasure is, there will your heart be also' (Matt. 6: 19–21). In English 'treasure' used to be an affectionate way for addressing a person you loved dearly; in Italian, '*tesoro*' still functions that way.

Revelation, Past, Present, and Future

In their 1963 Montreal report, the Faith and Order Commission showed that, to begin with, they were 'concerned primarily with the understanding of Tradition as it relates to the past, to the once-for-all event of Christ's coming in the flesh, his death and resurrection, and to the continuing work of the Holy Spirit within the Church'. But the Commission insisted that 'Tradition looks also to the present [the Spirit's 'continuing work'] *and to the future*' (emphasis added).[8] This reminds us that 'revelation' also has a triple time-key. To understand the past, present, and future function of tradition, we need to take into account what should be said about revelation then, now, and to come. Whatever precise form our terminology takes, we should distinguish between revelation (1) inasmuch as it reached an unsurpassable, once-and-for-all fullness with the life, death, and resurrection of Christ, the

---

[8] *Montreal 1963*, 87.

call of his apostles, and the outpouring of the Holy Spirit, (2) inasmuch as it continues today and calls people to faith in the living Christ, and (3) inasmuch as it will be gloriously and definitively concluded at the second coming of Christ. Revelation in one sense is past, in another sense is present, and in a further sense is a reality to come. The New Testament speaks in such a triple time-key of the divine self-revelation in Christ.

(1) First, the prologue of the Letter to the Hebrews announces a provisional and fragmentary revelation that led to a truly perfect and complete revelation: 'Long ago, God spoke to our ancestors in many and various ways to the prophets, but in these last days he has spoken to us by the Son' (Heb. 1: 1–2). Hebrews attributes the fullness of the divine revelation communicated through Jesus to his identity as *the Son of God*.

John's Gospel also understands the historical revelation through Christ as full and unsurpassable: 'the Word became flesh and pitched his tent among us, and we have seen his glory, the glory of the Father's only Son, full of grace and truth' (John 1: 14). In the logic of John's prologue, the divine revelation in and through Christ is full and complete, because he is *the Word of God*. To be sure, the language of sonship turns up in the same verse. This Gospel will go on to highlight Christ as the Son who reveals the Father (John 14: 9), and do so right through to the end when it sums up its central purpose: 'these things have been written so that you may come [or continue—alternative translation] to believe that Jesus is [revealed as—my editorial addition] the Messiah, *the Son of God*, and that through believing you may have life in his name' (John 20: 31). Yet, at least in the prologue, it is because he is the Word who 'was in the beginning', who 'was with God', and who 'was God' (John 1: 1) that he could communicate the fullness of 'grace and truth'.

Paul approaches the incarnational language of John when he writes in hymnic terms of the self-emptying and self-humbling involved in Christ 'being born in human likeness', 'being found in human form', and 'taking the form of a slave' before dying on a cross. This self-abasement led to the universal revelation that made it possible for 'every tongue to confess that Jesus Christ is Lord, to the glory of God the Father' (Phil. 2: 6–11). With their different accents, Hebrews,

John, and Paul converge in professing a past, divine self-revelation that was full, complete, and unsurpassable.

John of the Cross (1542–91), biblical scholar and mystic, brought out the implications of what the evangelist John had written. In his one and only Word, God has once and for all said everything to us, and now has nothing more to say. Jesus has proved not merely a revelation of God, but also *the* complete revelation of God: 'in giving us his Son, his one Word (for he [God] possesses no other), he spoke everything to us at once and in this sole Word—and he has nothing more to say'.[9] This famous comment on the divine self-revelation should not, however, lead us to ignore revelation as continuing to happen, a present state of affairs which Hebrews, the Johannine corpus, and Paul all attest.

(2) In a classic passage on faith, Hebrews states: 'now faith is the assurance of things hoped for, the proof of things not seen. By this [faith] the elders [our ancestors] received approval. By faith we understand that the universe was fashioned by the word of God, so that from what cannot be seen that which is seen has come into being' (Heb. 11: 1–3). Hebrews does not explicitly invoke the self-revealing activity of God that continues to give rise to faith. But it implies such revelation, notably by calling faith 'the proof of things not seen'. As C. R. Koester comments, 'the unseen realities of God give proof [present tense] of their existence by their power to evoke faith'.[10] The divine reality creates faith; the invisible power of God also evokes hope ('the assurance of things hoped for'). In other words, faith here and now is called into existence by the ongoing, revealing, proof-giving activity of God.

The Johannine corpus also represents revelation as happening here and now. The Book of Revelation, on the one hand, looks back to what Christ achieved and revealed (e.g. 1: 5–6, 17–18; 5: 9–10) and to those associated with him in that saving and revealing work, 'the apostles of the Lamb' (21: 14). On the other hand, Revelation

---

[9] John of the Cross, *Ascent of Mount Carmel*, 2.22.3; *The Collected Works of Saint John of the Cross*, trans. K. Kavanaugh and G. Rodriguez, rev. edn (Washington, DC: ICS Publications, 1991), 230.

[10] C. R. Koester, *Hebrews* (New York: Doubleday, 2001), 480.

represents the divine self-disclosure as happening here and now: for instance, in the messages that the risen and exalted Christ addresses through the Holy Spirit to seven churches in Asia. The faithful should listen in faith to 'what the Spirit is saying to them' right now (2: 1–3: 22).[11] Here divine revelation comes across as being a living event and continuing reality. Likewise, the First Letter of John, while it recalls how in the past 'the eternal life that was with the Father was revealed to us' (1: 2), 'testifies to' and 'declares' in the present what has been revealed (1: 1–3). The Johannine community accepts the past, divine self-revelation, and wants to convey it to another generation of present hearers and readers.

Paul expounds faith as the 'obedience of faith' given to God communicated through the apostolic preaching (Rom. 16: 26). The divine 'righteousness is revealed' to elicit the faith of human beings and bring them into a right relationship with God (Rom.1: 16–17). In a lyrical passage, the apostle portrays faith as responding to what is heard, 'the word of Christ' (Rom. 10: 14–17).[12] The good news that Paul preaches is nothing less than 'the [revealing] word of God' working to bring about faith and keep it alive (1 Thess. 2: 13). The heart of the apostolic preaching remains the resurrection of the crucified, the highpoint of divine revelation to which the believers look back and to which, in faith, they here and now continue to respond (1 Cor. 15: 3–11).

(3) Yet, thirdly, when Paul and other New Testament witnesses turn to the language of revelation, they slant it heavily towards *the future, divine self-manifestation* that will be the second coming of Christ, the fulfilment of the human race, and the end of all history.[13] Thus Hebrews announces that Christ 'will appear a second time' to 'save those who are eagerly waiting for him' (9: 28). First John comforts its readers with the promise, 'when he [God] is revealed, we shall be like him, for we shall see him as he is' (3: 2). Paul proclaims that 'the

[11] On these passages from Revelation, see C. R. Koester, *Revelation: A New Translation with Introduction and Commentary* (New Haven, CT: Yale University Press, 2014).

[12] On these passages from Paul, see J. A. Fitzmyer, *Romans* (New York: Doubleday, 1993).

[13] See A. Dulles, *Models of Revelation* (New York: Doubleday, 1983), 228–9.

revealing of the Lord' will be on 'the day of his final coming' (1 Cor. 1: 7–8), and reckons 'the sufferings of the present time' not 'worth comparing with the glory that will be revealed to us' (Rom. 8: 18).

Further New Testament witnesses disclose the same overriding tendency to link the language of revelation with the future. First Peter, while recognizing a past, divine self-disclosure when Christ 'was revealed at the end of the ages' (1: 20), repeatedly refers to the 'salvation ready to be revealed at the last time' (1: 3) and 'the grace that Jesus Christ will bring you when you are revealed' (1: 13; see 1: 7).[14] We find a similar tension between revelation as past and as future in the Letter to Titus. On the one hand, it rejoices that 'the grace of God has appeared, bringing salvation to all' (2: 11). On the other hand, two verses later it looks towards the future revelation: 'we wait for the blessed hope and the manifestation of the glory of our great God and Saviour Jesus Christ' (2: 13).

When the New Testament presents the divine self-communication as something that has happened (past) and something that will happen (final future), relatively few problems arise. *Difficulties concentrate on the present* and come from those who claim that any 'present revelation' is not revelation in the proper sense, but only a growth in the collective understanding of that revelation completed and 'closed' once and for all with Christ and his apostles. They sometimes appeal to Jude 3–4. The writer urges his readers to 'contend for the faith' against 'ungodly intruders who have perverted the [apostolic] faith that was once and for all entrusted to the saints'. Does this once-and-for-all entrusting of revelation imply that no further communication of revelation takes place, and that later generations of Christians merely have the task of remembering, interpreting, and applying the historical revelation? In other words, the claim is that here and now there is no 'living revelation', which would also mean that there is no 'living faith' and no 'living tradition'.

Undoubtedly a growth in interpreting and understanding revelation takes place. From a sociological point of view, Peter Berger comments on the experience of divine revelation prompting a

---

[14] On these passages from 1 Peter, see J. H. Elliott, *1 Peter: A New Translation, with Introduction and Commentary* (New York: Doubleday, 2000).

religious tradition that develops 'theoretical reflection', which accounts for and interprets the original experience.[15] *An Essay on the Development of Christian Doctrine* by Blessed John Henry Newman (1801–90) classically expounded the growth in collective understanding and interpretation that tradition has brought.[16] Nevertheless, we would not do justice to tradition, if, while accepting the development it has effected towards understanding past revelation, we denied that it continues to produce an actual revelation of God. The 1963 report of the Faith and Order Commission spoke of 'God's revelation and self-giving in Christ' as 'present in the life of the Church'. It is the witness of the Holy Spirit which brings it about that the past divine self-revelation recorded in the Scriptures is not only more fully understood but also constantly actualized as God's living revelation to the Church and through her to the world.[17]

To deny revelation in the present is to doubt the active power here and now of the Holy Spirit in guiding tradition and mediating the living presence of the risen Christ. It would also mean reducing faith to receiving some revealed truths, inherited from the past, rather than acknowledging faith in its integral, personal sense as being full obedience given to God revealed here and now through the living voice of the good news. In short, to deny present revelation of God also involves selling short its human correlative, faith.

To be sure, if one persists in holding that revelation entails *primarily* the communication of revealed truths *about* God (rather than the personal self-disclosure *of* God), it becomes easier to relegate revelation to the past. As soon as the whole set of revealed doctrines was communicated, revelation ended or was 'closed'. For this way of thinking, later, post-New Testament believers cannot immediately and directly experience revelation. All they can do is remember, interpret, and put into practice truths disclosed long ago to the apostolic Church.

Those who think this way should learn to recognize how present revelation (effected through the reading and proclaiming of the

---

[15] Berger, *The Heretical Imperative*, 52–3.

[16] J. H. Newman, *An Essay on the Development of Christian Doctrine*, 2nd edn (London: Longman, Green, & Co., 1878, 14th impression 1909; orig. edn 1845).

[17] *Montreal 1963*, 52; see the Second Vatican Council, *DV* 8.

Scriptures,[18] the Church's sacramental worship ('announcing the death of the Lord until he comes'—1 Cor. 11: 26), preaching, the witness of Christian living, and very many other means) *actualizes* the living event of the divine self-manifestation, and continues to do so in innumerable contexts and for those innumerable people who respond in faith. The past events and experiences which affected the chosen people, the prophets, Jesus, his apostles, and other founding fathers and mothers of Christianity are recalled and re-presented. God is not silent but continues to speak and call forth faith. Just as in the liturgy, the work of our redemption is continually exercised (*opus nostrae redemptionis exercetur*), so the work of divine revelation to us is continually exercised (*opus divinae revelationis exercetur*). This classic state-ment about the liturgical mediation of salvation *in the present* may be applied equally well to the liturgical (and extra-liturgical) mediation of revelation *in the present*: the work of revelation, the inseparable counterpart of salvation, is constantly 'exercised' or performed.

The present mediation of revelation (and salvation) depends essen-tially upon accepting the foundational and authoritative testimony about the past self-disclosure of God in Jesus Christ. Revelation, as believers experience and accept it now, derives from the witness of the apostolic generation. Their faith in and proclamation of the Gospel sprang from a special, immediate experience of Jesus during his lifetime and after his resurrection. The tradition of this apostolic testimony, which created the New Testament writings, continues to be determinative and normative for the post-apostolic tradition of Christians and their experience of God in Christ.

Here one must insist that ongoing, present revelation *does not add* to the essential 'content' of what was fully disclosed through Christ's life, death, resurrection, and co-sending of the Holy Spirit. As a living encounter with Christ through his Spirit mediated by the Church's tradition, this divine self-communication never stops. Yet this encoun-ter does not bring anything essentially new to what the apostolic generation came to know through their experience of Christ and his

---

[18] See how the Scriptures serve 'to instruct for salvation through [arousing] faith in Christ Jesus' (2 Tim. 3: 15). For an Ethiopian, a reading from Isaiah about the Suffering Servant, together with evangelization from Philip, brought him to faith in Christ and baptism (Acts 8: 26–40).

Spirit. There are no new truths to be added to the Nicene Creed or the Apostles' Creed.

Tradition as Process

As we have already seen, tradition often designates the living act or process of transmission (*actus tradendi*), an act that has taken indefinitely many forms in the history of Christianity: preaching, teaching (both through official leaders, theologians, and catechists), writing, celebrating the sacraments, interpreting the Scriptures through a *lectio divina* held in common, composing liturgical texts and hymns, creating sacred art, building churches and other ecclesial buildings, witnessing, like St Paul, through a Christ-centred life-style (1 Cor. 4: 16; 11: 1; Phil. 3: 17; 4: 9), making the *camino* to Santiago de Compostela or sharing in other pilgrimages, taking part in World Youth Days, and so forth. In a world of globalization and multiculturalism, the process of Christian tradition can also be furthered by the social media. As living actions, different forms of tradition constantly trigger 'moments of glad grace' (W. B. Yeats, 'When you are old'). The handing on of the good news, both in dramatic and seemingly ordinary ways, can bring a living sense of God's self-revelation and light up our existence.

Thus listening to the choir singing vespers on Christmas Day in the Cathedral of Notre-Dame (Paris) brought the light of faith to Paul Claudel (1868–1955). An unbeliever in his teenage years, he was changed for ever by that religious experience at the age of eighteen. Well over a thousand years earlier, hearing in church and putting into practice a text from Matthew 19: 21 ('If you want to be perfect, go sell all your possessions and give them to the poor, and come follow me, and you will have treasure in heaven') changed the life of a wealthy young Egyptian, St Antony of Egypt (d. 356). Deeply changed by hearing a traditional text being proclaimed, he contributed to the lasting story of Christianity by founding the eremitic monasticism of solitary hermits.[19]

We can distinguish at least *seven characteristics of tradition* as process. It is pre-given; we are collectively bound to tradition; it is richly

[19] On Antony and two similar cases, see O'Collins, *Revelation*, 207–14.

polymorphous; it shows a sacramental face; it can stand in tension with the reality we presently experience; it is constantly open to change and reform; and it belongs to a process that will end only with the close of human history.

Firstly, tradition is pre-given. In Chapter 1, we quoted Hans-Georg Gadamer using language that could have come from Edward Shils: tradition is 'the way we relate to the past' or the way the past is present. Hence 'we are always situated within traditions'; 'tradition is always part of us'.[20] We are born into a world shaped by a wealth of past practices and beliefs. As Christians we enter a community through the baptismal rite of initiation, a traditional ceremony that has existed from apostolic times. The letters of Paul and the Acts of the Apostles illustrate richly how the tradition of interpreting and preaching the Scriptures has characterized Christianity since the outset. In late December, very many Christians share a traditional practice introduced by St Francis of Assisi (d. 1226). By celebrating Christmas in a barn with animals and straw, he conveyed the deep meaning of Christ's birth and encouraged the widespread use of various figures to represent the nativity accounts with which the Gospels of Matthew and Luke begin. Human and Christian tradition embodies innumerable actions and objects that constitute the 'pre-givens' for the life of every human being and every Christian.

Second, tradition means that we find ourselves to be part of a common process. As Gadamer says, it is 'the communality that binds us to tradition'.[21] There is no such thing as the isolated tradition of an individual. Through tradition we enter a social process. We join others in singing the same carols during Advent and at Christmas. When individuals become Christians through baptism, they conform to the community, not vice versa. Tradition is always a common process, never a merely individual activity.

Third, there is huge diversity in the ways and means of God's self-revelation. The means of revelation range from tragically dramatic events like a crucifixion to sharing in sacred music led by an ancient orchestra (Ps. 150), pilgrimages to Jerusalem, and worship in the

---

[20] H.-G. Gadamer, *Truth and Method*, trans. J. Weinsheimer and D. G. Marshall, 2nd edn (New York: Crossroad, 1992), 282.

[21] Ibid. 293.

Temple.[22] The *polymorphous* nature of the processes that constitute Christian tradition matches that of the Old and New Testament revelation from which it came. A retired barrister who devoutly creates icons for churches and chapels in Melbourne, the singing of Mozart's *Krönungsmesse* in the Salzburg cathedral, and a committee of experts painstakingly composing a catechism for high school children in South Africa offer us just a few examples of the process of tradition in action. The sixteenth-century controversies over 'written and unwritten traditions' (Bettenson, 275–6; DzH 1501; ND 210) encouraged limiting the process of tradition to the transmission of the Scriptures and to word-of-mouth teaching that came from the apostolic Church but did not enter the books of the New Testament. The process of Christian tradition has been vastly richer than that.

Fourth, the living transmission that is the act of tradition consistently shows a *sacramental* structure. It blends words and intentional actions which work together sacramentally: as, for instance, the invocation of the Trinity lights up what is meant by the immersion in water or pouring of water in baptism. When creating hymns, composers old and new, like Charles Wesley (1707–88), Lucien Deiss (1921–2007), and Brian Wren (b. 1936), take biblical words and wed them to musical tunes. Pilgrimage as tradition also shows a sacramental form: something is done (by walking the distance to the goal, some holy place or shrine) and something also is said (the praying and spiritual exchanges with one's fellow pilgrims that belong essentially to the tradition of pilgrimages).

Sacraments are inseparably revealing and saving. What is said and done in administering the sacrament of baptism embodies the redeeming grace of Christ's death and resurrection. It also has a pedagogical function, in that it reveals the meaning of these words and actions. Likewise the processes of living tradition are simultaneously *revealing and saving*. The administration of baptism during the Easter vigil both informs and transforms not only the neophytes but also those participating in that liturgy.

The sacramental (word and deed) and revealing/saving nature of tradition derives from the origin of tradition in human beings

---

[22] O'Collins, *Revelation*, 66–72.

experiencing divine revelation. A passage from Vatican II's Constitution on Divine Revelation brings out the sacramental nature of revelation: it is communicated through 'deeds and words, which are intrinsically connected with each other', the 'works performed by God' and 'the words' that 'proclaim the works and elucidate the mystery they contain'. In the same passage Vatican II uses, more or less interchangeably, revelation and salvation. Revelation and salvation may be distinguishable but they are never separable. In Johannine terms, Christ is simultaneously 'the light of the world' (John 8: 5; 9: 5) and 'the life' of the world (John 14: 6). Hence *Dei Verbum* can shuttle back and forth between revelation and salvation:

> The economy of *revelation* takes place through deeds and words, intrinsically connected with each other. Thus the works performed by God in the history of *salvation* manifest and confirm the doctrine and realities signified by the words; the words, for their part, proclaim the works and elucidate the mystery they contain. The intimate truth, which this *revelation* gives us about God and the *salvation* of human beings, shines forth to us in Christ, who is both the mediator and the fullness of all *revelation*. (*DV* 2)

What was said here about revelation could legitimately be applied to the process of *Christian tradition* which comes from the experience of the divine revelation in Christ.

The economy of tradition takes place through deeds and words, intrinsically connected with each other. Thus the works performed by God through human agents in the history of tradition manifest and confirm the doctrine and realities signified by the words; the words of tradition, for their part, proclaim the works and elucidate the mystery they contain. The intimate truth, which this tradition gives us about God and the salvation of human beings, shines forth to us in Christ, who is both the mediator and the fullness of all tradition. Below we will return to the theme of Christ as mediator and fullness of tradition, the essential and central *Traditum*.

Fifth, prior traditions (found, for instance, in the language(s) one learns and the Bible one reads) condition, but obviously do not predetermine, all human and Christian understanding and interpretation. *Tensions* can emerge between some traditions and the present realities that one experiences. Peter Berger used 'heretical' as the opening word in the title of his now classical *Heretical Imperative* to highlight the choice (*hairesis*) that needs to be made between the claims of some traditions and those of experience.[23] At times the tensions between traditions and present realities are exacerbated by large-scale changes, such as the advanced industrialization, urbanization, and globalization of the 'runaway world' (see Anthony Giddens in Chapter 2 above). The disruptions of war and persecution may also trigger such tensions. What choices should Christians of ancient Middle Eastern churches make between their traditions and present realities, when they find themselves forced to flee to Canada, Australia, or other distant parts of the world?

Sixth, creative ideals and reforming zeal repeatedly lead to tradition being renewed and transformed in the light of present experience. Chapter 1 above has recalled how the Faith and Order Commission spoke of the need to deal with impoverished and even distorted traditions.[24] The Second Vatican Council spoke, more generally, of the Church 'always in need of purification' (*LG* 8) and 'constant reformation' (*UR* 6). This teaching about *ecclesia semper reformanda* implies a similar, constant *reformation* for traditions: *traditiones semper reformandae*. Reforming the Church inescapably means reforming traditions.

Seventh and finally, like revelation itself, Christian tradition will be gloriously and definitively concluded in the world to come. The process of tradition will continue, only to be completed and consummated at the end of all history. Unlike the canon of Scripture, a closed list of inspired books recognized as such by the Church, tradition is not canonically closed but remains an open-ended process that will reach closure only at the second coming of Christ.

Tradition as Object

Routinely, authors distinguish between tradition as a process (the *traditio* or *actus tradendi*) and the objects or object handed on. There are indefinitely many particular objects which are transmitted: the *tradita* or *traditiones*. Chapter 6 below will take up the task of

---

[23] Berger, *The Heretical Imperative.*   [24] *Montreal 1963*, 52.

discerning particular traditions, some of which can prove to be corrupt, impoverished, distorted, or simply outdated and needing to be dropped. The living process of tradition requires such change, but it can never amount to a complete rupture with the past. There will always be and necessarily be some measure of continuity along with discontinuity—as Edward Shils's study of tradition documents abundantly (Chapter 2 above).

The language of the Council of Trent about 'written and unwritten traditions' masked the very rich variety of *tradita* or particular traditions. Of course, one can classify many *human and Christian* traditions that way, but we need to put flesh and blood on any such summary: for instance, the written tradition of the Australian constitution that provided the basis for the federal union of six, sovereign states on 1 January 1901, as opposed to something that guards the southern approach to the city of Melbourne, the Shrine of Remembrance, an 'unwritten' monument constructed in honour of more than sixty thousand soldiers and others who died in the First World War. The *Imitation of Christ* by Thomas à Kempis (1380–1471), a pre-eminent example of written tradition, entered Christian history and became an enduringly popular expression of what a Christ-centred existence could be. In 1342 Franciscans took over an unwritten tradition, the custody of the shrines in Jerusalem associated with Christ's suffering and death. Those shrines were themselves already unwritten traditions. For Christians unable to visit the Holy Land, Franciscans and others erected innumerable Stations of the Cross, traditional means of sharing through prayer in the passion, death, and burial of Jesus. A Franciscan, St Leonard of Port Maurice (1676–1751), set up more than 500 sets of Stations, the most famous being those in the Colosseum of Rome, where popes have regularly led the faithful in prayer on Good Friday evening.

The next chapter will take up more examples of particular traditions or *tradita*. Can we also speak in the singular, of the *Traditum* or Tradition (in upper case) understood as the total, apostolic heritage of the Church or even personally as the risen Christ?

Here the Montreal report of the Faith and Order Commission, as we saw in Chapter 1, proves enlightening on the essential 'Traditum' (Tradition in upper case): 'Christ himself present in the life of the

Church'.[25] He is the ever-living Treasure (also upper case) at the heart of the Church, the Head of the Mystical Body who gives the Church its unity and graced existence. Understood as the *Christus praesens*, Tradition is 'not an object which we possess but a reality by which we are possessed'.[26] In the words with which Josef Geiselmann completed one of his books, Christ could say: 'I am tradition'.[27] 'The living Tradition', a theme cultivated in modern times by theologians of the Tübingen School, is the risen Christ, living yesterday, today, and forever (Heb. 13: 8).

It is a commonplace to observe how, for the Christian Church or any other community, tradition supplies their self-definition. Traditional narratives determine the identity of groups and individuals. In the case of Christianity, it is the central *Traditum, Christus praesens*, who determines the identity of his followers and supplies their essential self-definition.

Apropos of particular traditions (specific *tradita*), we cannot, without further examination, assert their normative and authoritative character and truth. Many long-standing traditions, such as a denial of freedom to those of other religious faiths (or of other Christians deemed to be 'heretics'), so far from enjoying normative permanence, have come to be seen as betraying the Gospel and so have been dropped. But in the case of the *Christus praesens*, the central *Traditum*, we face 'the' Norm, 'the' Authority, and 'the' supreme Truth. As the essential *Traditum*, handed on from one generation of Christians to another, he remains forever the *Way*, the *Truth*, the *Life* (John 14: 6).

Chapter 1 above recalled the 'total' nature of tradition as being the whole living heritage that is passed on. In the words of the Second Vatican Council's Constitution on Divine Revelation, 'what is handed on by the Apostles includes *everything* that contributes to making the People of God live their life in holiness and grow in faith. In this way, the Church, in her doctrine, life, and worship perpetuates and transmits to all generations *everything* that she herself is, *everything* that she believes' (*DV* 9; emphasis added). Without saying so, this passage points to the *Christus praesens*, handed on by the apostles through

---

[25] Ibid. 50.   [26] Ibid. 54.

[27] J. R. Geiselmann, *The Meaning of Tradition*, trans. W. J. O'Hara (Freiburg im Breisgau: Herder, 1962), 112.

fulfilling their missionary mandate (Matt. 28: 18–20). In person, he is 'everything' in the Church's 'doctrine, life, and worship' that 'makes the People of God live their lives in holiness and grow in faith'. By recognizing the *Christus praesens*, we are in a position to acknowledge him also as the great *Traditum* of Christian tradition.

The next chapter will attend further to particular traditions when we discuss the means and mediators of tradition. Before finishing this chapter, though, we need to advert, at least briefly, to the overlap between tradition and culture.

Culture

At the start of Chapter 2, we noted how Wolfhart Pannenberg, while ready at times to use the language of tradition, gave much more attention to questions of 'culture'. In a different context, the same preference showed up in the teaching of the Second Vatican Council. Its Constitution on Divine Revelation devoted one chapter of four articles to tradition (*DV* 7–10), while the Constitution on the Church in the Modern World devoted a longer chapter (ten articles) to Properly Promoting the Progress of Modern Culture (*GS* 53–62). All sixteen documents of Vatican II use '*traditio*' and '*traditionalis*' ninety-eight times, but use '*cultura*' and '*culturalis*' 128 times. Could one see in the case of both Pannenberg and Vatican II a muted, if limited, aversion to the language of 'tradition' as something burdensome and even a limit to freedom, an aversion that Edward Shils noted among social scientists (see start of Chapter 2)? Beyond question, a strong preference for culture over tradition continues to prevail not only in theological discourse but also in wider, academic circles. In the English language, there are at least thirty-nine academic journals currently in the area of cultural studies, with a Sage journal, *Theory, Culture & Society*, ranked number two. Titles illustrate how tradition languishes as a theme for research. Several journals are dedicated to 'traditional medicine', there is a quarterly, *Tradition: A Journal of Orthodox Jewish Thought*, and that seems to be all.

Undoubtedly, a certain equivalence shows up between tradition (which is always cultural and never natural) and culture. We can describe culture as the ideas, attitudes, and social behaviour of a given group of people.[28] Like tradition, culture helps to determine the identity of a group or society and supplies something of their essential self-definition. In all fields of culture, including the 'high culture' of arts and literature, tradition plays its role.

Tradition and culture—at least in a Christian context—pull apart over history, historical transmission, and action. First, built into the notion of Christian tradition is a sense of historical roots, of things being passed down through history, and then being modified or preserved for the future. Christianity is deeply and consciously rooted in (Old Testament) prophetic tradition and in (New Testament) apostolic tradition. The characteristic of 'apostolicity' in the Nicene Creed constantly recalls that Christianity must remain faithful to its *origins*, in the prehistory and history of Jesus Christ and his first followers. Tradition can be described as the collective memory of that past and its aftermath (see the appendix). When we talk about the 'traditional values' of a society or community, we are obviously talking with reference to historical origins and the historical practice of these values. If we speak of the 'cultural values' of a group or society, we do not necessarily interest ourselves in the past, formative process that created and transmitted these values. In short, a sense of historical roots and a collective memory of origins do not belong so readily to discourse about culture and living the values of one's culture.

Second, I might borrow from a philosopher friend of mine a brief version of traditions as 'ways of doing things', and perhaps expand this to talk of 'ways of doing things within a group or a whole society that are transmitted from one generation to the next'. Our inherited languages are ways of doing things with words. Pilgrimages, right

[28] See G. O. Lang, 'Culture', *New Catholic Encyclopedia*, iv, new edn (Washington, DC: Catholic University of America, 2003), 426–36; F. Rodi et al., 'Kultur', *TRE* xx, 176–209; B. J. F. Lonergan described 'a culture' as 'a set of meanings and values informing a common way of life' (*Method in Theology* (Toronto: University of Toronto Press, 1990), 301). Lonergan writes of tradition, but dedicates more than four times as much space to culture. In *Christ and Culture* (New York: Harper & Row, 1951), H. R. Niebuhr described culture, which he considered more or less synonymous with civilization, as 'that total process of human activity and that total result of such activity' (32). In passing, he called culture 'a social tradition' (57), but was so little concerned with tradition that it fails to feature in the index. He was a long way from writing a work entitled *Christ and Tradition*.

down to the World Youth Days initiated in 1986, are obviously ways of doing things with our bodies. With such physical structures as war memorials and cathedrals, we should join Edward Shils (see Chapter 2 above) in classifying them under 'tradition'. After all, cathedrals provide the setting for ways of doing things in worship as well as in sacred art and architecture. War memorials focus customary ways of doing things on 25 April (Anzac Day) and 11 November (Armistice Day). Written traditions, supremely the inspired Scriptures, record, interpret, and encourage ways of doing things as Jews and Christians.

Cultures undoubtedly concern ways of doing things. Niebuhr could even describe culture as 'that total process of human activity and the total result of such activity'.[29] But, in ordinary discourse, the firm alignment of 'culture' with shared ideas, attitudes, and values seems to take precedence over patterns of cultural behaviour. Tradition, especially when used and understood as process rather than as object, implies a closer link to ways of doing things. 'Culture' is not as such an 'action word', and so unlike 'tradition', and, for that matter, unlike other related action words like 'revelation' and 'inspiration'.

To an extent, tradition and culture overlap, but they are not synonymous and identical. Experiences of God created Jewish and Christian traditions. But we would be rightly hesitant about claiming, for example, that their experience of Jesus created the culture of the first Christians.

---

[29] See n. 26 above.

4

Transmission of Tradition, the *Sensus Fidelium*, and the Holy Spirit

Earlier chapters have already illustrated something of the astonishing variety both in the traditions that Christians have transmitted and in the identity of those engaged with this transmission (from bishops to the baptized faithful and, in some cases, those who follow other faiths or none at all). This chapter will begin by focusing on and demonstrating this variety, and conclude by reflecting on the Holy Spirit's role in transmitting the tradition—in particular, through the *sensus fidelium*, the faith instinct of the baptized.

The One *Traditum* and the Many *Tradita*

Christus praesens is the personal, living Tradition (upper case) preserved and transmitted at the heart of all Christian life. The presence of the crucified and risen Christ is actualized and expressed by innumerable traditions that may be earlier or later, simpler or more complex. Let me set out twelve such traditions (or groups of traditions) that embody or at least allude to the *Christus praesens*.

(1) By enacting a narrative of cleansing from sin, insertion into the life of Christ, and entrance into his family, baptism serves as the primary example of an ancient tradition that pushes back right to apostolic origins and, even earlier, to its anticipation in the practice of baptism by John. The reference of the baptismal tradition to Christ, the central *Traditum*, is too obvious to call for long documentation. Being baptized means being 'baptized into Christ', being 'clothed with Christ', and becoming 'one in Christ Jesus' (Gal. 3: 37–8).

At the start, it was through baptism 'in the name of Jesus' (Acts 2: 38)[1] that disciples knew their sins to be forgiven, received Christ's Holy Spirit, entered the community of the Church, and celebrated the Eucharist (1 Cor. 11: 23–6). Baptism 'in the name of the Father, *and of the Son*, and of the Holy Spirit' (Matt. 28: 19) rapidly became and remained the standard, traditional formula for the basic sacrament of Christian initiation.

(2) This trinitarian tradition of baptism provided the template for the Christian *creeds* that developed from the second century. Matthew 28: 19 ('baptizing them in the name of the Father, and of the Son, and of the Holy Spirit'), itself already a brief creedal tradition, offered a frame for forming longer Christian creeds: for instance, the Apostles' Creed and the Nicene Creed. The Apostles' Creed arose from a series of questions and answers that preceded baptism. This traditional creed has continued to be widely used at baptism and the Eucharist, but only in Western Christianity. The Nicene Creed—or, more accurately, the Nicene-Constantinopolitan Creed—is the product of the First Council of Nicaea (325) and the First Council of Constantinople (381). It is widely used during the Eucharist and at baptism, and is the most commonly accepted creed among all Christians. The World Council of Churches, formed at the first assembly in 1948, took this creed as its basic confession of faith in Jesus Christ. Thus two major doctrinal traditions have lasted and remain suitable for community worship today. This is an interesting case of one (biblical) tradition giving rise to other (post-biblical) traditions. In both cases, the parent tradition (in Matthew) and its classical offspring (the traditions of the Apostles' Creed and the Nicene Creed), the central *Traditum, Christus praesens*, is prominently recalled in the second article.[2]

---

[1] See C. S. Keener, *Acts: An Exegetical Commentary* (Grand Rapids, MI; Baker Academic, 2012), 972–86; J. A. Fitzmyer, *The Acts of the Apostles* (New York: Doubleday, 1998), 265–6.

[2] On the Nicene Creed, see W. Kinzig (ed.), *Faith in Formulae: A Collection of Early Christian Creeds and Creed-related Texts*, 4 vols (Oxford: Oxford University Press, 2017), i, 284–335; on the Roman Creed, the Apostles' Creed, and related Western texts, see ibid. ii, 221–441.

John E. Thiel rightly cites the creeds as significant elements of Christian tradition.[3] But he does not elaborate on the rich contribution that the creeds made and make to the Church's tradition, both in liturgy (mainly baptism and Eucharist) and in daily life.[4] Wolfram Kinzig gathers numerous examples of the creeds' place in the living tradition of the Church's liturgy and daily life. To enhance, for instance, the spiritual impact on pilgrims visiting the tombs of Saints Peter and Paul, Leo III (pope 795–816) used two silver shields on which the creed (probably the Nicene Creed) was inscribed, in the original Greek on one shield and in a Latin translation on the other. The shields were placed on the left and on the right of the entrance to Peter's tomb (under St Peter's Basilica). Only one shield, but of the purest silver, with the creed (in an unstated language) inscribed on it, was set at the entrance to the tomb of Paul (under St Paul's Outside the Walls).[5] These three shields linked a traditional creed with the two major apostles whose martyrdom witnessed to the *Traditum* at the heart of Christian faith, the *Christus praesens* himself. The shields joined two hardy traditions (pilgrimage and the veneration of Peter and Paul) with Christ, *the* Tradition in person.

(3) In the early Church, baptism (with its creedal confession of faith), confirmation (which has its roots in the coming of the Holy Spirit at the first Pentecost), and *the Eucharist* formed a single, interconnected process of Christian initiation. Convergent New Testament traditions about the Last Supper (1 Cor. 11: 23–6; Matt. 26: 26–9; Mark 14: 22–5; Luke 22: 14–20) supported the development of the Eucharist as the heart of the tradition and the Church's central act of worship.[6] Writing to the Corinthian Christians, Paul recalled the act of 'handing over' that began with Jesus himself and continued with Paul bringing them the Eucharist: 'I received from the Lord what I also handed on [*paredōka*] that the Lord Jesus on the night when he was handed over [*paredideto*] took a loaf of bread. And when he had

---

[3] J. E. Thiel, *Senses of Tradition: Continuity and Development in Catholic Faith* (New York: Oxford University Press, 2000), 32, 73, 130.

[4] For what the creeds contributed to the Church's life and liturgy from the fourth to the eighth century, see the entire fourth volume of Kinzig, *Faith in Formulae*.

[5] Ibid. 323–4.

[6] See B. D. Spinks, *Do This in Remembrance of Me: The Eucharist from the Early Church to the Present Day* (London: SCM Press, 2013).

given thanks, he broke it and said: "This is my body that is for you. Do this in remembrance of me"' (1 Cor. 11: 23–4).

An eloquent modern statement about the liturgical traditions actualizing the presence of the great *Traditum, Christus praesens*, has come from the Second Vatican Council:

> Christ is present in his Church, especially [*praesertim*] in her liturgical celebrations. He is present in the sacrifice of the Mass not only in the person of the minister... but supremely [*maxime*] in the eucharistic species. By his power he is present in the sacraments, so that when anyone baptizes it is really Christ himself who baptizes. He is present in his word, since it is he himself who speaks when the holy scriptures are read in the church. Lastly, he is present when the Church prays and sings. (*SC* 7)

This striking list of traditional, liturgical celebrations (the assembly of the baptized), the rites (the Eucharist, baptism, and other sacraments), persons (the ministers and others who take a specialized role in liturgies), and modes (reading of the Scriptures, as well as the singing and praying of the Church) that mediate the presence of Christ, the supreme *Traditum*, reaches its high point with the consecrated bread and wine upon the altar. There his fullest and most intense encounter with Christians combines with the other, traditional forms of presence (including his living and revelatory voice when sermons proclaim the good news (*SC* 33)), and reaches its summit in the sacramental communion of the liturgical assembly.

(4) Other Christian traditions began in post-apostolic times, such as the adoption of symbols previously used in civil ceremonies and then incorporated permanently into the liturgy for *Christian marriage*: for instance, the veil worn by the bride, her ring, and her joining hands with the bridegroom. Such traditional details have not unravelled with the passage of time, but have been preserved because they help sustain the identity of Christian marriage and its connection with Christ himself.[7]

---

[7] See P. L. Reynolds, *Marriage in the Western Church: The Christianization of Marriage During the Patristic and Early Medieval Periods* (Leiden: E. J. Brill, 1994); Reynolds, *How Marriage Became One of the Sacraments* (Cambridge: Cambridge University Press, 2016); K. W. Stevenson, *Nuptial Blessing: A Story of Christian Marriage Rites* (London: Alcuin Club, 1982).

Even if it took many centuries before Christians recognized the precise sacramental status of marriage, they had deeply linked it to Jesus in various ways. He drew images from weddings for some of his parables (e.g. Matt. 21: 1–14; 25: 1: 13). John's Gospel reports how Jesus attended a wedding at the start of his public ministry (John 2: 1–11); the other Gospels show how Jesus strove to safeguard the institution of marriage. He wanted to restore God's original plan for a married partnership expressed in the story of creation (Gen. 2: 18, 24). Hence Jesus excluded divorce and remarriage as contrary to the divine will. The traditional marriage rite preserves his saying, 'what God has joined together let no one put asunder' (Mark 10: 9 parr.).[8]

New Testament Christians recognized the *Christus praesens* to be their divine Spouse; collectively, they were united to him like a wife to a perfectly loving husband (e.g. Rev. 21: 9). The Letter to the Ephesians appeals to the great 'mystery' of the union of all the baptized with Christ, in order to encourage a startlingly elevated view of the loving relationship between Christian wives and husbands (Eph. 5: 25–33).

St Augustine of North Africa seems to have been the first Christian writer (in 401) to state the purpose and nature of matrimony. He wrote not only of 'offspring [*proles*]' but also of 'fidelity [*fides*]' and 'mutual consent [*sacramentum*]' (*De Bono Coniugali*, 3). He could exploit the fact that the Latin word *sacramentum* not only denoted the act of legal consent but also corresponded to the meaning of 'mystery' in Ephesians 5: 32. For Augustine, the 'mystery' of the love of Christ (the divine Spouse) for his bride (the Church) must be related to the tradition of Christian marriage.

(5) We should not skip over Christian traditions that existed in ancient times and were eliminated or quietly dropped—only to be later regenerated. Here I can call to witness the Prayer of the Faithful (also called Common Prayer) and the Rite of Christian Initiation of Adults (the RCIA).

An instruction on prayer in 1 Timothy urged that 'supplications, prayers, intercessions, and thanksgiving be made for everyone, for kings and all who are in high positions' (2: 1–2).[9] Early Christian liturgies included such a Prayer of the Faithful, but, at least in the Roman rite, it disappeared except for the intercessions found in the Good Friday liturgy. Footnoting the two verses in 1 Timothy as its scriptural warrant, the Second Vatican Council mandated the restoration of the Prayer of the Faithful, at least for Sundays and holy days of obligation (*SC* 53). The retrieval of this liturgical tradition has proved overall a notable success, and has often been extended to the celebration of weekday liturgies.

1 Timothy provided at once a link to the *Christus praesens* by adding: 'there is one God, there is also one Mediator between God and human kind, Christ Jesus, himself human, who gave himself as a ransom for all' (2: 5–6). The earlier Letter to the Romans had already attributed the exercise of heavenly intercession to the crucified and risen Jesus: enthroned at God's right hand, he constantly 'intercedes for us' (8: 34). According to Hebrews, Christ's mediatorial priesthood continues for ever, inasmuch as he 'lives always' to 'make intercession' for those who 'approach God through him' (7: 25).[10] By taking up once again in the traditional Prayer of the Faithful, Christians join themselves with the one Mediator, Christ the unique *Traditum*, in interceding for all people.

We can celebrate also the vitality of another ancient tradition that fell into abeyance but was restored, thanks to Vatican II (*SC* 64). A course of preparation for adults who wish to be baptized and enter the Catholic Church, the catechumenate was introduced (or rather re-introduced after many centuries) in 1972 in the form of the RCIA. Once enrolled as catechumens, the candidates are instructed in the faith and obligations of Christians—normally during the six weeks of Lent.[11] From the third to the fifth Sunday of Lent, they undergo 'scrutinies', or soul-searching examinations of conscience, so

[9] L. T. Johnson, *The First and Second Letters to Timothy* (New York: Doubleday, 2001), 188–90, 195–6.

[10] C. R. Koester, *Hebrews* (New York: Doubleday, 2001), 366, 371–2.

[11] In the opening rite of acceptance into the order of catechumens, the RCIA tradition links the candidates with the gospel of Christ, after which the sign of Christ's cross is traced on their forehead (*The Rites of the Catholic Church*, i A (New York: Pueblo Publishing Company, 1988), 55–9).

that they can detect their weaknesses and pray to be delivered from them. Those undergoing these demanding exercises are supported by the prayers of the community. At the Easter Vigil, they receive the sacraments of baptism, confirmation, and Eucharist—thus following as adults the traditional order of Christian initiation, one ceremony in which the candidates were baptized, confirmed, and received Holy Communion, in an utterly Christ- and Trinity-centred sequence.

(6) Some Christian traditions are relatively simple, like the central ceremony of *Ash Wednesday*. On the first day of Lent, the Roman rite, which is generally used in the West, offers a penitential service during which the faithful receive ashes on their forehead or on the crown of their heads. They are exhorted: 'turn away from sin and be faithful to the gospel', or 'remember you are dust and to dust you will return'.[12] Fidelity to the Gospel evokes the good news that is Christ, the new Adam who has overcome death in person.

Other traditional objects, such as the *palms* used on Palm Sunday, feature in slightly more complex ceremonies. A feast celebrated by all Christians at the start of Holy Week (or the Great Week as the Greek Orthodox call it) commemorates the final entry of Christ into Jerusalem when people waved or spread leafy branches in front of him (Mark 11: 8 par.). It is one of the twelve major feasts of the Eastern Orthodox calendar, preceded by Lazarus Saturday, which recalls Christ raising Lazarus from the dead (John 11: 1–44). The Western liturgy of Palm Sunday begins with the blessing and distribution of the palms and a procession; in the Eucharist itself, the passion story, according to Matthew, Mark, or Luke, is read. From the end of the fourth century, Egeria the Pilgrim reports the already traditional celebration in Jerusalem of Palm Sunday,[13] a feast that derives all its meaning from Christ, the living heart of Christian tradition.

---

[12] On the origin and meaning of 'Ash Wednesday', as well as the origin and meaning of the traditional use of candles, holy water, hymns, incense, palms (on Palm Sunday), and plainsong, see the relevant entries in F. L. Cross and E. A. Livingstone (eds), *The Oxford Dictionary of the Christian Church*, 3rd edn (Oxford: Oxford University Press, 2005).

[13] *Egeria's Travels*, trans. J. Wilkinson, 3rd edn (Warminster: Aris and Phillips, 1999).

(7) The tradition of palm branches goes back to the history of Jesus. Other traditional usages, such as singing (psalms) and using musical instruments (e.g. Ps. 150) reach back even earlier. Traditions of sacred music drew communities together in glorifying and encountering God and so being transformed, collectively and individually.[14] Martin Luther, himself a notable composer, held that, next to the Word of God, music is the greatest gift to humankind.[15]

Another, related tradition, the use of sweet-smelling *incense*, also reaches back to rites followed in the Jerusalem Temple (e.g. Ps. 141: 2). The scented smoke of burning incense that rose to God meant squandering something costly as a gift of unconditional love. Incense has maintained a central place in the worship of Orthodox Christians. Western Catholics use it frequently in processions, in the celebration of the Mass, for benediction of the Blessed Sacrament, and at funerals. The reference of incense to *Christus praesens* comes through powerfully, when, as regularly happens, a central cross or crucifix, the altar (an ancient symbol of Christ), the Book of the Gospels, and the Blessed Sacrament are solemnly incensed.

Other traditions are ancient but not quite as old: for instance, the use of *holy water* or blessed water. From at least the fourth century, it has entered such religious ceremonies as funeral services and the penitential rite at the beginning of the Eucharist, and signifies spiritual cleansing and dedication (as does the water blessed and used in baptism). Holy water summons up the Christ-centred symbolism of water attested by John's Gospel (John 7: 37–9; 19: 34). *Christus praesens*, the essential *Traditum*, is the true water to whom all such traditions as that of holy water allude.

---

[14] See three books by J. S. Begbie: *Music, Modernity and God: Essays in Listening* (Oxford: Oxford University Press, 2013); *Resounding Truth: Christian Wisdom in the World of Music* (Grand Rapids, MI: Baker Academic, 2007); *Theology, Music and Time* (Cambridge: Cambridge University Press, 2000). See also S. A. Reily and J. M. Dueck (eds), *Oxford Handbook of Music and World Christianities* (Oxford: Oxford University Press, 2016); D. Saliers and E. Saliers, *A Song to Live, a Life to Live: Reflections on Music as Spiritual Practice* (San Francisco: Wiley, 2005); Z. Sheridan, *Tamil Folk Music as Dalit Liberation Theology* (Bloomington: Indiana University Press, 2013); and J. M. LeMon, 'Symphonizing the Psalms: Igor Stravinsky's Musical Exegesis', *Interpretation* 71 (2017), 25–49.

[15] See P. Westermeyer, 'Music', in T. J. Wengert et al. (eds), *Dictionary of Luther and the Lutheran Traditions* (Grand Rapids, MI: Baker Academic, 2017), 527–9.

The use of *candles* belongs to another ancient, widespread tradition. Church ceremonies are regularly accompanied by lighted candles. Day and night a light, usually a lighted candle, burns before the tabernacle containing consecrated hosts. The life of Catholic Christians unfolds from a candle received at baptism, through a First Communion candle, to the Paschal Candle alight at their burial. At the Easter Vigil, this (large) Paschal Candle is lit and carried into the church by the celebrant. He sings three times '*Lumen Christi* (the Light of Christ)', and shares the light with the congregation, who hold small candles. When the faithful visit a church, they often light a votive candle in front of the statue of a favourite saint.

In the East, Christians light candles in front of icons of the Trinity, Christ, and his angels and saints. At the entrance or narthex (Greek for 'antechamber') of Eastern churches, there are usually stands for votive candles. The *manoualia*, or large candlesticks in front of the icon-ostasis, are lit for the Eucharistic liturgy, along with three candles (on the altar) for the Trinity and twelve candles (for the twelve apostles) on one (or several) candelabras. Candles from the Good Friday celebration are taken home and kept, much as Western Catholics take palms home on Palm Sunday. Traditionally, candles symbolize complete dedication or 'burning oneself out' in the service of Christ and his community. In various ways, the tradition of candles in Eastern and Western Christianity relates to Christ, the central *Traditum* of all Christianity.

(8) Mention of Eastern churches recalls the *traditional rites* of Eastern Christians, which involve considerable differences not only in worship but also in the whole style of life for a particular church with its specific spirituality and discipline. *Rite* in this sense coincides with the whole tradition (or all the *tradita*) of a given church: that is, with the liturgical, spiritual, theological, and disciplinary patrimony enjoyed by a self-governing church. Among Eastern Christians, there are now seven such major rites: the Armenian, the Byzantine, the Coptic, the East-Syrian (sometimes called Assyro-Chaldean), the Ethiopian, the Maronite (or Syro-Maronite), and West-Syrian (or Antiochene). These seven rites are found in both the Catholic and Orthodox traditions, except for the Maronite rite, which is only Catholic.[16]

[16] Abundant information about these rites can be found in Cross and Livingstone (eds), *The Oxford Dictionary of the Christian Church*; G. O'Collins and E. G. Farrugia, *A Concise Theological Dictionary*, 3rd edn (Mahwah, NJ: Paulist Press, 2013); and D. Patte

No theology of tradition should ignore the traditional Eastern rites or churches. Vatican II's Decree on the Eastern Catholic Churches of 1964, *Orientalium Ecclesiarum*, sets a good example here. It contains much on tradition, with the noun form of *traditio* appearing twelve times in this relatively short text of thirty articles. When praising the traditions of the Eastern Churches, the decree also speaks of the Eastern 'heritage [*patrimonium*]' interchangeably with 'tradition' (art. 1, 3, 5). The particular traditions and rites of Eastern Christianity yield a pluriform witness to the central *Traditum*, Christ himself.

(9) From the fourth century, traditions of *religious institutes* emerged and have been handed on—forms of existence for Christian men and women who practise evangelical poverty, chastity, and obedience, and follow a common life under a superior. In Eastern Christianity, religious men and women live mainly in monasteries; in the West, Dominicans, Franciscans, Jesuits, and other active religious orders have offered an alternative to a strictly contemplative monastic life. The traditions of religious life, which belong squarely to the central *tradita* of Christianity, embody and pass on deep experiences of the Son of God that led men and women like St Francis of Assisi and St Clare centuries ago into founding the religious communities that bear their names. The enduring power of such traditions was symbolized by the choice of title made by Pope Francis for an encyclical letter on ecology and climate change.[17] He took his title from the words of a canticle in which the Christ-like Francis of Assisi 'reminds us that our common home [the earth] is like a sister with whom we share our life and a beautiful mother who opens her arms to embrace us' (art. 1).

Here we should not forget the multitude of lay Christians who have inherited and contributed to *traditions of caring* for the sick and elderly, helping the poor, teaching children, and serving others in many 'social ministries'. Such traditions continue in modern times through groups who run soup kitchens, staff leprosaria, provide the homeless with

---

(ed.), *The Cambridge Dictionary of Christianity* (New York: Cambridge University Press, 2010). For longer accounts, see R. Roberson, *Eastern Christian Churches*, 6th edn (Rome: Pontifical Oriental Institute, 1999).

[17] *Laudato Si'* (Vatican City: Libreria Editrice Vaticana, 2015).

clothes and shelter, create family communities for the intellectually disabled, champion the cause of asylum seekers, serve refugees, and the rest. Those who engage themselves in such social ministries have drawn inspiration from the teaching of Christ (Matt. 25: 31–46; Luke 10: 25–37; 16: 19–31) and also from the specific traditions of the groups which they have joined: for instance, the Order of Malta (founded in Jerusalem in the eleventh century), the Vincent de Paul Society (founded in Paris in the mid-nineteenth century), and the San Egidio community (founded in Rome in 1968). Particular traditions of Christian service, along with institutional forms of religious life, reveal and transmit the reality of *Christus praesens*, the *Traditum* at the heart of all Christian living and serving.

(10) Christian traditions also encompass *painting, sculpture, mosaics, tapestry*, and *architecture*, with wonderful results that are still with us.[18] Here we take up *building programmes* that have served to hand on faithful witness to the living Christ.

Let me recall examples from Rome, from Monreale, Chartres, and elsewhere. A visit to the basilica of St Mary Major leaves the deepest impression on some visitors to Rome—not least through the sweep of Christian tradition it incorporates. In a square outside, the fluted column that carries a seventeenth-century statue of the Virgin Mary came from a fourth-century public building constructed by the Emperor Constantine. Completed in 440, the interior of the basilica retains its traditional magnificence. Thirty-six marble columns and four granite ones divide the nave from the aisles, and the whole building follows the style of a Roman basilica or hall for public administration. Exquisite fifth-century mosaics along the nave and over the triumphal arch depict scenes from the stories of Old Testament patriarchs, the life of Moses, and the early life of Jesus. Down to the nineteenth century, generations have added their statues, pavements, mosaics, chapels, altars, tombs, and the rest. St Mary Major incorporates Christian tradition from the fifth to the nineteenth century, a tradition that continues to witness to Christ and his saints.

A twelfth-century mosaic sets the Virgin Mary on a throne alongside her Son, and recalls how the Council of Ephesus in 431 defended

---

[18]   See e.g. Guntram Koch, *Early Christian Art and Architecture*, trans. John Bowden (London: SCM Press, 1996).

her traditional title of *Theotokos* or Mother of God (see 'the Mother of my Lord' in Luke 1: 43). What one sees in St Mary Major witnesses to various episodes in the tradition of the Church and history of the world. For instance, the basilica houses the first figures ever made for a Christmas crèche or crib, those created by Arnolfo di Cambio and his assistants (late thirteenth century). The elaborate ceiling, gilded with what is traditionally said to be the first gold brought back from the Americas by Christopher Columbus and presented to Alexander VI (pope 1492–1503) by Ferdinand V of Aragon (1452–1516) and Isabella of Castile (1451–1504), evokes the grim and glorious story of the conquest of the Americas. Along with St Mary Major, many other church buildings in Rome illuminate Christian tradition—not least the basilica of St Agnes on the Via Nomentana.[19]

Church buildings from the eleventh to the sixteenth century bear traditional witness to Christianity of those centuries, when all classes of society conspired to express their faith in *Christus praesens* through mosaics, carvings, paintings, stained-glass windows, and the magnificent churches and monasteries that housed them. From round AD 1000 until the thirteenth century, Romanesque style (and its variant in Norman style) dominated—with massive walls, relatively small windows, and round arches and vaults. The Romanesque basilica of Vézelay (south-east of Paris) and the Norman (with Arab decoration) Abbey of Monreale (near Palermo in Sicily) offer outstanding examples from those centuries. The twelfth-century mosaics of the Abbey of Monreale represent an entire cycle of Old Testament and New Testament stories and figures, with a gigantic Christ conferring his blessing and enthroned in the central apse.

The tradition of Gothic style began with the rebuilding of the royal abbey church of Saint-Denis (near Paris), which was dedicated in 1144. Pointed arches, soaring towers, and the light that streamed through the walls of stained glass lifted believers' minds and hearts to God. The Gothic cathedrals of Chartres (begun 1145) and Amiens (begun 1220) became models for churches right across Europe. The rich sculpture, stained glass, and luminous structure of Chartres Cathedral (south-west of Paris) have always inspired superlatives.

---

[19] See Margaret Visser's precious volume, *The Geometry of Love* (New York: Farrar, Straus & Giroux, 2000).

It is Christian tradition witnessing at its best to Christ. A descendant of two American presidents, Henry Adams (1838–1918), wrote in *Mont-Saint-Michel and Chartres*: 'if you want to know what churches were made for, come down here on some great festival of the Virgin and give yourself up to it, but come alone! That kind of knowledge cannot be taught and can seldom be shared.'[20] Charles Péguy (1873–1914), who died at the front in the opening weeks of the First World War, helped to maintain the tradition of Chartres Cathedral as a goal for modern pilgrimages. Its forty-four window groupings depict a vast array of Old Testament and New Testament scenes; its hundreds of carved figures express Christian life and faith in a traditional and very lifelike way.

Tourists become pilgrims at the Basilica of St Mary Major, the Abbey of Monreale, and Chartres Cathedral. These buildings are not merely enduring monuments of human culture. They are eloquent witnesses to the heart of Christian tradition, *Christus praesens*.

We have pointed to different examples taken from Christian tradition: baptism, creeds, the Eucharist, marriage symbols, the Prayer of the Faithful, the RCIA, ashes, palms, music, incense, holy water, candles, the Eastern rites, religious institutes, lay groups engaged in social ministries, and cathedrals and other church buildings. These traditional forms all contribute to the rich, living tradition of the Church—something that I missed in Thiel's account. He mentions the developing dogma of the *Immaculate Conception* of the Blessed Virgin Mary and the emergence of the *Baroque* style.[21] But in his treatment these remain intellectual, doctrinal matters. One misses the exuberant celebration of the feast, the tender beauty of paintings by Murillo, and all the other traditional items that made the Immaculate Conception a deeply cherished theme in the living tradition of the Church. Likewise, Thiel contented himself with merely speaking of the Baroque 'mentality', and remained silent about the liturgical celebration, music, architecture, painting, and sculpture that established the Baroque movement as a compelling and vital presence in seventeenth- and eighteenth-century Catholic life in Europe, Latin America, and

---

[20] H. Adams, *Mont-Saint-Michel and Chartres* (New York: Doubleday, 1959), 117.
[21] Thiel, *Senses of Tradition*, 13, 23, 93–4.

elsewhere. As someone who lived for over thirty years in a city enriched forever by the sculpture and architecture of Gian Lorenzo Bernini (1598–1680), I found a mere nod towards the Baroque input into tradition less than satisfactory.

(12) Finally, it is at our peril that we neglect a central tradition which has been passed on since the birth of Christianity: the Holy Scriptures themselves. The ancient Codex Sinaiticus and Codex Vaticanus, the even earlier Chester Beatty and Bodmer papyri, the defence mounted by Irenaeus against attempts to eliminate the Old Testament, the knowledge of the Bible shown by the sermons and other works of Augustine of Hippo, and the carvings, mosaics, and stained-glass windows that told the biblical stories—all witness to the Church's concern to preserve and transmit the entire Bible. The inspired Scriptures and their inspired witness to *Christus praesens* belong at the heart of Christian tradition, as the four-volume *New Cambridge History of the Bible* demonstrates abundantly.[22]

Dated from around 800, the glorious writing and illustrations of the Book of Kells (from a monastery in County Meath but now housed in Trinity College Dublin) present the four Gospels. The Book of Kells attests the monastic love for the Scriptures in general and for Christ and his life in particular. It implies that finally the Bible has only one truth to proclaim, the personal disclosure of the triune God in Jesus Christ, a revealing story told in fourfold form by the evangelists Matthew, Mark, Luke, and John. The Bible is the unique (written) *Traditum* that has been handed on by the Christian Church (in the original languages and through innumerable translations) and that points to the unique (personal and life-giving) *Traditum*, the crucified and risen Jesus.

A twelfth-century Augustinian canon, Hugh of St Victor, witnessed to this union of the Bible with Christ: 'all divine Scripture speaks of Christ and all divine Scripture finds its fulfilment in Christ . . . because all divine Scripture forms one book, which is the book of life'.[23] In the sixteenth century, William Tyndale expressed the same conviction: 'the scriptures spring out of God, and flow into Christ, and were given

---

[22] J. C. Paget et al. (eds) (Cambridge: Cambridge University Press, 2012).
[23] *De Arca Noe Morali*, 2. 8–9, *PL* 176, cols 642–3.

to lead us to Christ. Thou must therefore go along by the scripture as by a line, until thou come to Christ, which is the way's end and resting place.'[24]

Few items in traditional, liturgical practice express more vividly the biblical presence of Christ than the custom of rising to greet the Book of the Gospels, incensing it, reverencing it, and raising it to bless the assembled faithful. A custom that went back at least to the fifth century involved enthroning the Book of the Gospels at councils, so as to symbolize the presiding presence of the risen Christ.[25] As used in liturgical and extra-liturgical traditions, the Book of the Gospels continues to prove a particular tradition that vividly points to and enables the presence of Christianity's central *Traditum*, the crucified and risen Christ, the living and life-giving Tradition at the heart of the Church.

The Transmitters of Tradition

When we turn to explore the groups and individuals that share in the post-New Testament transmission of tradition, we plunge into the task of naming a vast army of official and unofficial witnesses. Popes, patriarchs, bishops, priests, deacons, councils (both general and local), synods (in both the Eastern and Western churches), parish priests, faculties of theology, monasteries and other religious houses (along with their individual members), catechists, teachers, health-care workers (and the institutions they staff), those who work for the Christian media, and innumerable lay persons exercise some major or minor official role in handing on the traditions that make up the worship, belief, and practice of the Church. Thus, for their children, 'Christian couples' are 'the first heralds and teachers of the faith'; they transmit the faith 'by word and example'.[26]

---

[24] *The Work of William Tyndale*, ed. G. E. Duffield (Philadelphia: Fortress Press, 1965), 353.

[25] R. de Maio, *The Book of the Gospels at the Oecumenical Councils* (Vatican City: Biblioteca Apostolica Vaticana, 1963).

[26] The Second Vatican Council, Decree on the Apostolate of Lay People (*Apostolicam Actuositatem*), 11.

From the time of the Council of Jerusalem (Acts 15: 1–29), *Church councils* rank pre-eminent for officially transmitting the Christian tradition. Their *traditio activa* becomes *traditio passiva*, as conciliar teaching is remembered, developed, and applied by later general councils and lesser groups of official teachers. By collecting conciliar, papal, and other important teaching in chronological or topical order, three volumes listed above among the abbreviations, Bettenson/Maunder, Denzinger/Hünermann, and Neuner/Dupuis, have furthered such official transmission of Christian faith.

But we should not neglect the *unofficial transmitters* of tradition. Since the birth of Christianity, through their individual gifts a host of witnesses have handed on the treasure of the faith through their writing, hymns and other musical compositions, painting, sculpture, and architecture. They cannot establish their role as transmitters of Christian tradition by producing such official documents as certificates of ordination, marriage, or appointment to theological faculties. But, while official transmitters of tradition can fail in their task, gifted, unofficial individuals have, by the test of time, established themselves as hugely influential in passing on the Christian tradition. I think here of the *Divine Comedy* of Dante Alighieri (d. 1321), the sculptures and paintings of Michelangelo Buonarroti (d. 1564), the poetry of George Herbert (d. 1633) and Gerard Manley Hopkins (d. 1889), and the music of Johann Sebastian Bach (d. 1750). Along with them belong a multitude of anonymous artists and builders who worked on such monuments of tradition as the Basilica of St Mary Major, the Abbey of Monreale, and Chartres Cathedral. Here I think also of a friend Geoffrey, who has passed on the Christian faith through his gift in creating icons; he has enriched at least seven churches or chapels in Melbourne with icons of Christ, his Mother, martyrs, and other saints.

Let us not forget the thirty-six *doctors of the Church*, like Athanasius of Alexandria, Augustine of Hippo, and Teresa of Avila. They became such through their personal charisms and not through any kind of official appointment. Their writings continue to expound and pass on the good news to generation after generation of readers. The witness of their lives also played a major role in transmitting the Christian tradition.

We cannot make too much of *saintly men and women* whose lives glow like jewels in the history of the human race and who have led the way in handing on the treasure of faith in Christ. Inspired by St Vincent de

Paul (1581–1660) and St Louise de Marillac (1591–1660), generations of men and women have dedicated themselves to the needs of the sick and the poor. The witness of St Francis of Assisi (d. 1226) and St Clare (d. 1253) continues to make them outstanding transmitters of the Christian tradition. Teaching in Rome right through the pontificate of St John Paul II (1978–2005), I was deeply impressed by his decision to bring home to the world the testimony of holiness by beatifying or canonizing many heroic men and women. Before he died, the Pope had canonized or declared to be saints 482 men and women, and had also beatified—a stage before possible canonization—a total of 1338. Many of those beatified or canonized died a martyr's death, including 103 Koreans whom he canonized on a visit to Seoul in May 1984. On 1 October 2000, he canonized 120 men and women who had been martyred in China from the seventeenth to the twentieth century.[27]

In 7 May 2000, John Paul II led an ecumenical prayer service at the Colosseum, the place where tradition placed the death of many early Christian martyrs. The Pope wanted to recall the much larger number of Christians who in *the twentieth century* had suffered and died for their faith. That ceremony recalled with honour Dietrich Bonhoeffer (d. 1945), Oscar Romero (d. 1980), and numerous other men and women (Anglican, Catholic, Orthodox, and Protestant), who around the world witnessed to their common faith through imprisonment and death. Dedicated disciples of Jesus do not have to be beatified or canonized to transmit the tradition of Christian faith through the powerful witness of their words and deeds.[28]

The *Sensus Fidelium* and the Holy Spirit

Even if not yet with full clarity, Irenaeus of Lyons (d. around 200) appreciated how the Holy Spirit is the primary bearer of the Church's tradition and life. His principle, 'where the Church is, there is the

[27] On John Paul II beatifying and canonizing numerous saintly men and women, see G. O'Collins, *On the Left Bank of the Tiber* (Brisbane/Leominster: Connor Court/Gracewing, 2013), 136–43.

[28] On the persecution that continues, see John L. Allen, *The Global War on Christians: Dispatches from the Front Lines of Anti-Christian Persecution* (New York: Random House, 2013).

Spirit of God' (*Adversus Haereses*, 3. 24. 1), formed a sound starting point that followed on from the promise of Jesus, 'the Spirit of truth will guide you into all truth' (John 16: 13). This being guided into truth does not happen apart from the risen and glorified Christ, the essential *Traditum* of Christianity. Rather one should envisage the Holy Spirit transmitting the truth of tradition by actualizing the union with Christ of all the baptized faithful. In Paul's terms, it is the Spirit of the Son who 'has been sent into the hearts' of believers (Gal. 4: 6).

Hence the apostle can pray for the whole community of Colossae 'that you may be *filled with the knowledge [epignōsis] of God's will* in all *spiritual wisdom [sophia] and understanding [sunesis]*, so that you may lead lives worthy of the Lord [Jesus Christ], fully pleasing to him, as you bear fruit in every good work and you *grow in the knowledge [epignōsis] of God*' (Col. 1: 9–10).[29] Growing in and being filled with this wisdom, understanding, and knowledge of—or better, 'insight into'—God and the divine will came to be summed up as the *sensus fidelium* (the sense of the faithful). Being faithful to the traditional apostolic message requires the baptized to have insight into their faith, so that they can understand, interpret, and practise it worthily and fruitfully, through the wisdom that comes from the Spirit.

The Letter to the Ephesians pictures the situation of Gentiles who have not yet accepted the Gospel: 'they are darkened in their understanding [*dianoia*], alienated from the life of God because of their ignorance [*agnoia*] and hardness of heart' (Eph. 4: 18). The faithful baptized have left behind this situation:

> [I pray] that the God of our Lord Jesus Christ, the Father of glory, may give you a spirit of wisdom [*sophia*] and of revelation in the knowledge [*epignōsis*] of him, so that, with the eyes of your heart enlightened, you may know what is the hope to which he has called you, what are the riches of his glorious inheritance among the saints, and what is the

---

[29] See how, in a similar vein, Paul prays for a broader audience: 'I want their hearts to be encouraged and united in love, so that they may have all the riches of full understanding [*sunesis*] and have insight [*epignōsis*] into the mystery of God, that is, Christ himself, in whom are hidden all the treasures of wisdom [*sophia*] and knowledge [*gnōsis*]' (Col. 2: 2–3). On these verses and on Col. 1: 9–10, see M. Barth and H. Blanke, *Colossians: A New Translation with Introduction and Commentary* (New York: Doubleday, 1994), 173–80, 275–83.

immeasurable greatness of his power for us who believe, according to
the working of his great power.   (Eph. 1: 17–19)[30]

The divine 'revelation' has prompted the faith (of 'us who believe'),
which, blessed by the Spirit of wisdom, sees 'with the eyes of the heart'
and knows the 'glorious inheritance' that has been handed on to the
faithful believers.

The longest Pauline passage about what would be called the *sensus
fidelium* comes from 1 Corinthians 2: 9–16.[31] The apostle explicitly
mentions the Holy Spirit six times, and assures his readers that 'we
have received the Spirit that is from God, so that we may understand
the gifts bestowed upon us by God. And we speak of these things in
words not taught by human wisdom but taught by the Spirit, interpreting spiritual things for those who are spiritual' (1 Cor. 2: 12–13).
Receiving the Spirit and being 'taught by the Spirit', the whole
community, and not just its leaders, share a spiritual awareness.
They are all in a position to understand, interpret, and hand on
what has been bestowed on them.

The Second Vatican Council, while converging with the 1963
conference of the Faith and Order Commission by presenting in its
Constitution on Divine Revelation (*Dei Verbum* of 1965) the Holy Spirit
as the One who guarantees the whole Church's essential fidelity in
transmitting the tradition (see Chapter 1 above), preferred to speak,
not of the *sensus fidelium*, but twice of the supernatural *sensus fidei* (the
sense of faith) that 'is aroused and sustained by the Spirit of truth'
(*LG* 12). In a section on promoting the well-being of married and
family life, however, the Council's Constitution on the Church in the
Modern World, *Gaudium et Spes* (Joy and Hope), appealed to 'the
Christian sense of the faithful [*sensus fidelium*]' (*GS* 52). The two expressions are roughly equivalent, with *sensus fidei* suggesting perhaps more
clearly that faith and its 'sense' have 'come' (Gal. 3: 25) as gifts of
the Spirit.[32] The extensive ecumenical dialogues and practical

---

[30] On these verses, see E. Best, *Ephesians* (London: T. & T. Clark, 1998), 161–70.

[31] On these verses, see J. A. Fitzmyer, *First Corinthians* (New Haven, CT: Yale
University Press, 2008), 179–86; and A. C. Thiselton, *The First Epistle to the
Corinthians* (Grand Rapids, MI: Eerdmans, 2000), 248–86.

[32] See G. Koch (ed.), *Mitsprache im Glauben? Von Glaubenssinn der Glaübigen* (Würzburg:
Echter, 1993); O. Rush, *The Eyes of Faith: The Sense of the Faithful and the Church's Reception*

collaboration that arose with Vatican II suggest attending to the 'sense of faith' that the Spirit of truth has 'aroused and sustained' in other, baptized Christians.[33] Chapter 6 will face the questions: What have other Christians learned from the Holy Spirit in their worship, doctrinal perspectives, and living practice? What might Catholics learn from them (and others) in discerning and reforming their traditions?

Here let me end by emphasizing the way in which the activity of the Holy Spirit underpins the *sensus fidelium*. Let me take up two examples to illustrate how the Spirit 'comes to our help in our weakness' in prayer and beyond (Rom. 8: 26).

First, the Eucharist, the heart of Christian tradition, includes a twofold *epiclesis* or invocation, the first placed before and the other after the words of institution. The former prays that the Holy Spirit may descend upon the gifts to change them into the body and blood of Christ for the spiritual profit of those who receive them. The latter invocation asks that the Spirit descend upon the assembled faithful and transform them.

My second example (briefly cited in Chapter 1) comes from the ordination of bishops, essential figures in the transmission of tradition, and puts on display their human weakness and need for constant help from the Holy Spirit. The prayers used in the ceremony highlight abundantly how they require the guidance of the Spirit—above all the prayer of ordination itself. During that prayer, two deacons hold the Book of the Gospels above the head of the candidate—a sign of the new bishop's desire to live and proclaim the message of Jesus Christ. But that will happen only through being enabled by the power of the Spirit, *the* Transmitter of the central *Traditum, Christus praesens* himself. It is in and through the Holy Spirit that the *sensus fidelium* becomes and remains operative in all the members of the Church.

---

of Revelation (Washington, DC: Catholic University of America Press, 2009); J. J. Burkard, 'The *Sensus Fidelium*', in G. Mannion and L. S. Mudge (eds), *The Routledge Companion to the Christian Church* (New York and London: Routledge, 2008), 560–75.

[33] O. Rush, 'Receptive Ecumenism and Discerning the *Sensus Fidelium*: Expanding the Categories for a Catholic Reception of Revelation', *Theological Studies* 78 (2017), 559–72.

5

Tradition and Scripture

The Council of Trent by a decree of 8 April 1546 (Bettenson 264–5; DzH 1501–9; ND 210–15) proposed one Gospel and two modes of its communication, Scripture and tradition, with God revealing truth and working for the salvation of human beings through both modes. The rise of historical consciousness and developing insights into hermeneutics (or the art of interpretation) allow us to take a broader view and see how, in the two thousand years of Christianity, Scripture and tradition have worked together in mutual dependence. Gerhard Ebeling, looking at this story, could interpret the history and heritage of the whole Christian Church as the history and heritage of the exposition of the Scriptures.[1] The four-volume *New Cambridge History of the Bible*[2] encourages us to sum up tradition as the reception or 'effective history' (*Wirkungsgeschichte*) of the Bible—the way in which Christian believers and their leaders interpreted and applied the Bible through their worship, systems of belief, and entire practice of life. The living tradition interpreted the Scriptures but was also interpreted and challenged by the Scriptures. These are the headlines; let us now move to some of the small print.

Creeds, Adam/New Adam, and Justification

We might sum up the Scriptures as the written, prophetic (Old Testament) and apostolic (New Testament) testimony to the divine

---

[1] G. Ebeling, *The Word of God and Tradition*, trans. S. H. Hooke (London: Collins, 1968), 11–31.

[2] J. C. Paget et al. (eds) (Cambridge: Cambridge University Press, 2012); see also such specific studies as J. A. Schroeder, *The Bible in Medieval Tradition: The Book of Jeremiah* (Grand Rapids, MI: Eerdmans, 2017).

self-communication that reached its highpoint with the incarnation, life, death, and resurrection of the Son of God (along with the coming of the Holy Spirit). Out of traditions that incorporated and interpreted memories of the divine activity and self-disclosure, the sacred writers produced the inspired texts that would shape the teaching and life of the post-New Testament church. Let us take three examples to illustrate this process: the creeds, the figures of Adam and Eve, and justification by faith.

(1) In his *Catecheses*, St Cyril of Jerusalem (d. 386) explained to his baptismal candidates the nature of the faith enshrined in the *creeds*, at that point in history notably the Nicene Creed of 325 and the Apostles' Creed or Old Roman Creed (that emerged in the fourth century): 'memorize the creed as I recite it, and you will receive in due course the proof from Scripture of each of its propositions. For not according to man's pleasure have the articles of faith been comprehended, but the most important points collected from the Scriptures make up the complete teaching of the faith' (5. 12).[3]

What Cyril did not mention here to his baptismal candidates was the sharp and even fierce discussion about the biblical language assembled to form the Nicene Creed in response to the challenge of Arius (d. around 336), who held the Son of God to be strictly inferior to and infinitely different from the Father.[4] Against Arius and his followers, the orthodox quoted Johannine texts that set Christ on a par with God: 'I and the Father are one' (John 10: 30; see 10: 38; 17: 21–2). In arguing for Christ's subordinate position, the Arians retorted by citing John 14: 28 ('the Father is greater than I'), and explained away John 10: 30 as pointing only to Jesus' always acting

---

[3] *The Works of Saint Cyril of Jerusalem*, trans. L. P. McCauley and A. A. Stephenson, i (Washington, DC: Catholic University of America Press, 1969), 146. On the creeds, see Bettenson, 25–8; J. N. D. Kelly, *Early Christian Creeds*, 3rd edn (London: Longman, 1972); W. Kinzig (ed.), *Early Christian Formulae: A Collection of Early Christian Creeds and Creed-related Texts*, 4 vols (Oxford: Oxford University Press, 2017); E. Lanczkowski et al., 'Glaubensbekenntnis(se)', *TRE* xiii, 384–446; F. E. Vokes et al., 'Apostolisches Glaubensbekenntnis', ibid. iii, 528–71.

[4] See L. Ayres, *Nicaea and its Legacy: An Approach to Fourth-century Trinitarian Theology* (Oxford: Oxford University Press, 2004); R. Williams, *Arius: Heresy and Tradition* (London: Darton, Longman & Todd, 1987).

and speaking in harmony with the Father and the divine will. The orthodox dealt with the 'subordination' of John 14: 28 by referring it simply to Jesus in his incarnate life on earth. But for both sides the central question remained: What does a faithful interpretation of the Scriptures—and, in particular, of the four Gospels—say about the being of Christ?

In speaking out clearly for the divinity of Christ, the bishops at the First Council of Nicaea used only biblical terms in the Creed that they endorsed, with the exception of the adjective *homo-ousios* ('of one being' with the Father). The term had a chequered background and was open to misinterpretation.[5] Nevertheless, as an adjective connected with the verb *eimi*, it hinted at the majestic self-presentation of God in Exodus 3: 14: *egō eimi* ('I am'). One may not dismiss *homo-ousios* out of hand for being non-biblical.

Neither the Apostles' Creed nor the Nicene Creed (in its fuller form from the 381 First Council of Constantinople) was developed as a substitute for the Scriptures. Candidates for baptism and already initiated members of the Church found in these creeds normative frames of reference to guide their Christian understanding of the tripersonal God and the missions of the Son and the Holy Spirit for human salvation. The two creeds borrowed from the Scriptures language with which to summarize the biblical message about the Trinity.[6] Often set to music, they became a permanent part of the liturgical tradition of the Church and shaped her appropriation of the Scriptures.

---

[5] See G. O'Collins, *Christology: A Biblical, Historical, and Systematic Study of Jesus*, 2nd edn (Oxford: Oxford University Press, 2009), 184–5.

[6] In a review (*Theology* 121 (2018), 68–70) of my *Revelation: Towards a Christian Interpretation of God's Self-revelation in Jesus Christ* (Oxford: Oxford University Press, 2016), Mark Ord raises the interesting question of distinguishing between 'the cognitive content' of the proposition 'Jesus is Lord' as found in the New Testament (e.g. 1 Cor. 12: 3) and as found in the Nicene Creed. On the one hand, there is some basic identity (about the divine status and authority of Jesus) in the meaning of the proposition in the two contexts. On the other hand, the full cognitive context of the proposition will be affected by the particular experiences of New Testament Christians (starting with Paul himself) and the millions of believers who have recited the Creed down through the centuries. Even among the first Christians there never was such a thing as THE identical cognitive content of the proposition 'Jesus is Lord'.

(2) In a major contribution to Christology, St Paul contrasted *Adam and Christ* as two corporate personalities or representatives (Rom. 5: 12–21; 1 Cor. 15: 20–3, 45–9) and understood human beings to bear the image of both Adam and Christ (1 Cor. 15: 49). Where the disobedience of Adam meant sin and death for all, Christ's obedience, through bringing righteousness and an abundance of grace (Rom. 5: 12–21), more than made good the harm caused by Adam. As a 'life-giving spirit', the last Adam is risen from the dead and, through resurrection into a heavenly, spiritual existence, will transform the redeemed (1 Cor. 15: 22, 45, 48–9). Paul's Adam Christology involved both the earthly Jesus' obedience (Rom. 5) and the risen Christ's role as giver of the Spirit (1 Cor. 15). An explicit Adam Christology seems to have been introduced by Paul himself—first in 1 Corinthians 15 and then in Romans 5.[7]

In the second century St Irenaeus (d. around 200) did much to shape a tradition of receiving and developing Paul's antithetical parallelism between Adam and Christ, with the latter more than reversing the failure of the former and Mary joining her Son as the new Eve. In a typical passage from his *Adversus Haereses*, Irenaeus wrote: 'The Son of God...was incarnate and made man; and then he summed up (recapitulated) in himself the long line of the human race, procuring for us a comprehensive salvation, that we might recover in Christ Jesus what in Adam we had lost, namely the state of being in the image and likeness of God' (3. 18. 1).

When developing his scheme of Adam/Christ, Irenaeus joined Paul in citing the teaching of Genesis. Hence he rejected the way a second-century heretic, Marcion (d. around 160) excluded all the Jewish Scriptures as coming from a powerful but evil God of the Old Testament. Irenaeus relied on Genesis as a book of divine origin to picture the obedient Christ as the New Adam (and Mary as the obedient New Eve). Controversy marked this beginning of a post-New Testament tradition that interpreted and elaborated Paul's teaching about Christ as Second Adam. But controversy did not normally attend the subsequent development of this traditional interpretation.[8]

---

[7] See J. A. Fitzmyer, *Romans* (New York: Doubleday, 1993), 136, 406, 412.

[8] The tradition reached a recent highpoint with the Second Vatican Council's Pastoral Constitution on the Church in the Modern World. It cited the language of

Taking up Paul's insight and interpreting Christ as the 'second' or 'last' Adam, who 'reran' a programme and more than made up what had failed in Adam and Eve, became a lasting item in the Church's tradition: in the teaching of Origen (d. around 254), St Hilary of Poitiers (d. 367), St Athanasius of Alexandria (d. 373), St Gregory of Nazianzus (d. 389), St Gregory of Nyssa (d. 395), and other Church fathers.[9] Some linked Adam (from whose side God formed Eve according to Gen. 2: 21–2) to Christ as the new Adam by interpreting the piercing of Christ's side on the cross (with the subsequent flow of water and blood (John 19: 34) that symbolized baptism and other 'mysteries') to constitute the birth of the Church. Just as Eve was formed from the side of Adam while he was in a deep sleep, so the Church was formed from Christ when he was in the sleep of death.[10] By referring twice to Adam, the *Exultet* or Easter proclamation, a liturgical text which can be traced to the fourth century, implied Christ's role as Last Adam.[11] The Latin poet Venantius Fortunatus (d. around 610) in a hymn *Crux fidelis* ('faithful cross') vividly transposed Paul's contrast of the two Adams by setting the tree from which Adam and Eve took the forbidden fruit over against Christ's cross as the tree of life. The preface for the feast of the Holy Cross or Exaltation of the Cross (14 September), a feast that goes back at least to the seventh century, follows suit: 'death came from a tree, life was to spring from a tree'. Those semi-liturgical celebrations, which were the medieval Mystery Plays, highlighted the connection between the two Adams by the practice of having the same actor portray Adam and then return as Christ.[12]

---

the Letter to the Ephesians about all things being 'recapitulated' in Christ (*GS* 45), presented the New Adam as 'saving all people and recapitulating all things', and backed up this teaching with appropriate references to Irenaeus (*GS* 57).

[9] See P. B. Ely, *Adam and Eve in Scripture, Theology and Literature* (Lanham, MD: Lexington Books, 2018); and S. Greenblatt, *The Rise and Fall of Adam and Eve* (London: Bodley Head, 2017).

[10] See e.g. St John Chrysostom (d. 407), *Catecheses*, 3. 13–19.

[11] See E. H. Aubert, 'Exultet', *Encyclopedia of the Bible and Its Reception*, viii (Berlin: De Gruyter, 2014), 553–5.

[12] See further R. Woolf, *The English Mystery Plays* (Berkeley, CA: University of California Press, 1980); and B. Murdoch, *Adam's Grace: Fall and Redemption in Medieval Literature* (Cambridge: D. S. Brewer, 2000).

In the sixteenth century, Martin Luther and other Reformers made original sin a matter of debate and controversy. The Council of Trent cited Romans 5 when proposing the doctrine of Adam's sin, its effects, and its transmission to the descendants of Adam and Eve (DzH 1511–14; ND 508–11). More than four centuries later, the Second Vatican Council (1962–5), without quoting explicitly Romans 5 but in what would become one of the most valued passages of the Pastoral Constitution on the Church in the Modern World, presented Christ as the New Adam (*GS* 22). The 1992 *Catechism of the Catholic Church*, when drawing on modern biblical scholarship to reformulate Trent's decree on original sin, took up Romans 5 specifically (art. 397, 400, and 402).[13]

For centuries, Christian literature has followed the insight of Paul by connecting Adam and Christ. In a 'Hymn to God my God in my Sickness', John Donne (d. 1631) wrote:

> We think that Paradise and Calvary,
> Christ's cross and Adam's tree, stood in one place;[14]
> Look, Lord, and find both Adams met in me;
> As the first Adam's sweat surrounds my face,
> May the last Adam's blood my soul embrace.[15]

Another outstanding comment on the Genesis story and Paul's linking of the two Adams turned up several decades later in *Paradise Regained* by John Milton (d. 1674). After expanding the story of Adam and Eve into the twelve books of *Paradise Lost*, Milton focused the four-book sequel entirely on the temptation in the wilderness. Unlike Adam and Eve, the Second Adam succeeds in resisting temptation.

---

[13] *The Catechism of the Catholic Church* (Vatican City: Libreria Editrice Vaticanan, 1994).

[14] An old and enduring legend told the story of the tree from which Adam and Eve took the forbidden fruit, and described how it eventually became the tree of Calvary on which Christ died. According to a related legend, Calvary was the place where Adam was buried; Christian artists at times placed his skull, and occasionally even his skeleton, at the foot of the cross. Some artists pictured Adam and Eve standing together in a sarcophagus under the cross. In a few representations Adam holds a chalice to receive the blood falling from Christ on the tree. See G. Schiller, *Iconography of Christian Art*, trans. J. Seligman, ii (London: Lund Humphries, 1972), 130–2.

[15] *John Donne*, ed. J. Carey (Oxford: Oxford University Press, 1990), 332.

Literature and music have kept alive the tradition inspired by Paul's linking and contrasting Adam and Christ: from Blessed John Henry Newman's *Dream of Gerontius* ('a second Adam to the fight and to the rescue come'), set to music by Sir William Elgar (d. 1906), down to James McAuley (d. 1976; 'By your kingly power, O risen Lord, all that Adam lost is now restored; in your resurrection be adored'), a poem set to music by Richard Connolly (b. 1927).

Paul's commentary on the Genesis story linked creation, which reached its climax with the making of the original Adam and Eve, with redemption effected by the Second Adam. The human condition in its glory and misery is symbolized by Adam and Eve. After being created in the image and likeness of God, they lapsed into sin and were driven out of paradise. The tradition of Eastern iconography has maintained and expanded the Adam/Christ link. Icons show the last Adam on Holy Saturday descending into the dark pit of the underworld and releasing from their long bondage Adam, Eve, and innumerable others waiting for redemption in the 'limbo of the fathers'. In some of these icons Christ carries the wooden cross on which he died, and so can remind Christians of the tree from which Adam and Eve took the forbidden fruit.

(3) A third example illustrating the mutual impact of Scripture and the tradition of interpretation also comes from Paul's letters: *the doctrine of justification*.[16] According to the major Protestant Reformers, original sin had so deeply damaged our human nature that we remain steeped in sinfulness and commit sin in every action.[17] Martin Luther and Jean Calvin used strong, even lurid, language about our depravity. But there is room for a generous reading that seems closer to what they intended and, for that matter, to what Catholic saints and certain outstanding biblical figures (e.g. Isa. 6: 1–7) have sometimes said

[16] See A. E. McGrath, 'Justification', in H. J. Hillerbrand (ed.), *The Oxford Encyclopedia of the Reformation*, ii (New York: Oxford University Press, 1996); R. Saarinen, 'Justification by Faith: The View of the Mannermaa School', in R. Kolb et al. (eds), *The Oxford Handbook of Martin Luther's Theology* (Oxford: Oxford University Press, 2014), 254–63; M. Mattes, 'Luther on Justification as Forensic and Effective', ibid. 264–73.

[17] See L. Batka, 'Luther's Teaching on Sin and Evil', ibid. 233–53; K.-H. zur Muhlen, 'Sin', *Oxford Encyclopedia of the Reformation*, iv, 61–5.

about their own human weakness and wickedness. The closer we draw to God in our spiritual lives, the more we become aware of and even terrified by the overwhelming divine holiness that rises infinitely above our tainted and limited nature.

How then can God's justifying grace reach us sinners?[18] Luther preached that Christ's righteousness is legally ascribed or imputed (rather than imparted) to us. Internally we remain sinners but externally we are 'acquitted' by God through Christ's redeeming merits.

A solemn Catholic response to Luther came late and appeared a year after his death, when the Council of Trent produced its decree on justification in 1547 (Bettenson 266; DzH 1520–83; ND 1924–83).[19] A document of sixteen chapters, summarized in thirty-three 'canons', it constantly invokes or echoes the Scriptures—not least Paul's letter to the Galatians, the letter to the Romans, and the two letters to the Corinthians. Trent clearly intended to take its stand on what God revealed in Christ about the life of grace—a revelation recorded and interpreted in the Scriptures. Trent approached the task of presenting the biblical message of justification after centuries of traditional teaching produced in different contexts: opposition to Pelagianism (which taught that human beings could achieve salvation through their own sustained efforts), the pessimism which characterized views adopted by the older Augustine, the more optimistic interpretation of the human condition developed by Thomas Aquinas, and many other developments (including the questions and challenges coming from the Reformers themselves).

In summary, Trent joined Paul in highlighting the gratuitousness and relational character of God's grace. The Tridentine decree, therefore, agreed with Luther and other Protestant Reformers by acknowledging the utter primacy of divine love and saving power in the whole process of justification. Even if human beings can reject the illumination of the Holy Spirit, by their own free will they cannot 'take

---

[18] See D. S. Yeago, 'Grace', *Oxford Encyclopedia of the Reformation*, ii, 184–9.

[19] W. Joest, 'Die tridentinische Rechtfertigungslehre', *Kerygma und Dogma* 9 (1963), 41–69; A. E. McGrath, *Iustitia Dei: A History of the Christian Doctrine of Justification*, 3rd edn (Cambridge: Cambridge University Press, 2005); J. W. O'Malley, *Trent: What Happened at the Council* (Cambridge, MA: Belknap Press of Harvard University Press, 2013), 107–16, 253–4, 262, 306–7.

one step towards justice in God's sight'. They must always be 'awakened and assisted by divine grace, if they are to repent of their sins and be reborn through baptism' (DzH 1525–6; ND 1929–30). The righteousness that makes human beings acceptable to God comes through faith in Christ and not through any human works. When human beings accept the divine grace, they do so through the very gift of God.

The Tridentine decree on justification differed from what Luther and other Reformers understood the Scriptures to say. According to Trent, the grace received through baptism intrinsically transforms or regenerates sinners through the power of the Holy Spirit. Justification brings not only 'the remission of sins' but also an interior 'sanctification and renewal through the voluntary reception of grace' (DzH 1528; ND 1932).

Although often seen as mutually exclusive, the Catholic and Lutheran approaches to the Pauline teaching on justification may be interpreted as complementing rather than contradicting each other. Despite significant differences in terminology and emphases in those approaches, advances in biblical and historical scholarship have made a consensus possible. In 1967 the international Catholic–Lutheran theological dialogue began. Three decades later, its 'Joint Declaration on the Doctrine of Justification', which contains forty-four common statements covering basic tenets regarding justification, was accepted by the Catholic Church and the World Lutheran Federation and signed in Augsburg on 31 October 1999.[20] Some differences still remain: for instance, about the interplay between divine grace and human freedom. But a substantial agreement has now been reached on a doctrine (and the interpretation of Paul's letters to the Galatians and Romans), which once divided the Christian Church.[21] Since 1999, the World Methodist Council, the World Community of

---

[20] The text is found in *Origins* 28 (1998), 120–7.

[21] See D. E. Aune (ed.), *Rereading Paul Together: Protestant and Catholic Perspectives on Justification* (Grand Rapids, MI: Baker Academic, 2006); J. K. Beilby and P. R. Eddy (eds), *Justification: Five Views* (Downers Grove, IL: IVP Academic, 2011); Peter Matheson, 'Luther on Galatians', in M. Lieb, E. Mason, and J. Roberts (eds), *Oxford Handbook of the Reception History of the Bible* (Oxford: Oxford University Press, 2011), 621–34; John Riches, 'Galatians', ibid. 149–60.

Reformed Churches, and the Anglican Consultative Committee have all endorsed the Joint Declaration on the Doctrine of Justification. It provided a central theme for the ecumenical service in Westminster Abbey, London, held on 31 October 2017 to commemorate Luther's publishing his 95 theses five hundred years earlier and triggering the Reformation.

Religious Freedom

The temptation has often been overwhelming to superimpose prefabricated theories when explaining the interplay of Scripture and tradition. This approach only makes us drift further away from the life of the Christian Church where this interplay, often characterized by much tension, works itself out in practice. A couple of concrete examples, taken from Vatican II's teaching on religious freedom and on a Christian relationship with the Jewish people, throw contemporary light on the power of Scriptures to correct long-standing, false traditions.

In a Declaration on Religious Freedom, *Dignitatis Humanae*, promulgated on 7 December 1965, the Catholic Church 'finally abandoned the traditional doctrine that "error has no rights" and embraced a more liberal theory based on the rights of the person, and the individual's duty to follow his conscience'.[22] An article that appeared in the Turin-based daily paper, *La Stampa*, spoke not of the Church 'abandoning' a 'traditional doctrine' and 'embracing a more liberal theory' but of a development of doctrine: 'the schema which deals with religious freedom constitutes by itself a genuine development of doctrine, perhaps the greatest and most characteristic progress achieved by the Council'.[23]

---

[22] Basil Mitchell, 'The Christian Conscience', in John McManners (ed.), *The Oxford Illustrated History of Christianity* (Oxford: Oxford University Press, 1990), 602 27, at 602–3.

[23] Quoted by Pietro Pavan, 'Declaration on Religious Freedom', in Herbert Vorgrimler (ed.), *Commentary on Vatican II*, iv (London: Burns & Oates, 1969), 49–86, at 62. On the making of *DH*, see Silvia Scatena, *La fatica della libertà: l'elaborazione della dichiarazione 'Dignitatis Humanae' sulla libertà umana del Vaticano II* (Bologna: Il Mulino, 2003).

The anonymous author of the *La Stampa* article took up the language of Vatican II itself. In teaching the right of individuals to religious liberty—that is to say, their freedom in civil society to worship God according to their conscience—the Council announced that it intended 'to develop [*evolvere*] the teaching of more recent popes about the inviolable rights of the human person and about the juridical regulation of society' (art. 1). The declaration ended by endorsing religious freedom, 'the greatest of the duties and rights of human beings' (art. 15). When, however, we recall how the *Syllabus of Errors*, published by Pius IX in 1864, excluded public religious freedom, how could Vatican II allege that its declaration represented a development in official teaching? In a footnote that accompanied article 2, *Dignitatis Humanae* cited prior teaching by John XXIII (d. 1963), Pius XII (d. 1958), Pius XI (d. 1939), and Leo XIII (d. 1903). But, pointedly, it did not attempt to enlist any support from Pius IX. The 'more recent popes' stopped at Leo XIII (pope 1878–1903). *Dignitatis Humanae*, when set over against the *Syllabus of Errors*, looks more like a reversal than a development of doctrine.[24]

In the *Syllabus of Errors*, Pius IX had condemned the proposition that 'everyone is free to embrace and profess the religion which by the light of reason one judges to be true' (DzH 2915; ND 1013/15). Compare this with the statement from *Dignitatis Humanae* that 'the human person has the right to religious freedom' (*DH* 1). The *Syllabus* rejected the notion of the Catholic Church surrendering or losing its position when it enjoyed a monopoly as the state church, and so condemned the proposition: 'in our age, it is no longer advisable that the Catholic religion be the only state religion, excluding all the other cults' (DzH 2977; ND 1103/77). For *Dignitatis Humanae*, however, 'the other cults' were not 'to be excluded' in countries where the Catholic Church or any other religious group was constitutionally recognized: 'if, in view of the particular circumstances of peoples, special recognition is assigned in the constitution to one religious community, the right of all citizens and religious communities to freedom in religious matters must at the same time be recognized and respected' (*DH* 6).

---

[24] See F. A. Sullivan, 'Catholic Tradition and Traditions', in M. J. Lacey and F. Oakley (eds), *The Crisis of Modernity in Catholic Modernity* (New York: Oxford University Press, 2011), 113–33, at 126–7.

What has prompted the change of teaching from the *Syllabus of Errors* to *Dignitatis Humanae?* The latter document mentions three reasons, which culminate with some decisive teaching from the New Testament.

Firstly, *Dignitatis Humanae* shows itself ready to respect the widespread 'desires' for the free exercise of religion in society. The Council 'declares' these desires to be 'in conformity with truth and justice' (*DH* 1). Later the declaration observes not only that 'people of today want to be able to profess their religion in public and in private', but also that 'religious liberty is already declared a civil right in many constitutions and solemnly recognized in international documents' (*DH* 15).There is an obvious reference here to article 18 of the 1948 Universal Declaration of Human Rights: 'Everyone has the right to freedom of thought, conscience, and religion; this right includes freedom to change his [*sic*] religion or belief, and freedom, either alone or in community with others and in public and in private, to manifest his religion or belief in teaching, practice, worship and observance.' One motive for the change of teaching introduced by *Dignitatis Humanae* is the desire to catch up with the true and just concerns of contemporary humanity.

Second, in the spirit of retrieving a valuable past, the Council also announced its intention to 'examine the sacred tradition and doctrine of the Church, from which it produces new things always consistent [*congruentia*] with the old' (*DH* 1).[25] Obviously the declaration produced something strikingly 'new' (in official Roman Catholic teaching) by insisting that governments should safeguard religious freedom. But what could 'the old things' be that were consistent with this new teaching on religious freedom? They were certainly not 'old things' authorized by the *Syllabus of Errors*, but rather things that *Dignitatis Humanae* recognized as known 'through the revealed word of God and reason' (*DH* 2). A later article in the declaration reversed this order: 'the demands [of human dignity] have become more fully known to *human reason* through the experience of centuries'. Furthermore, 'this

---

[25] Talking of *nova et vetera* conjures up the implied signature of the author of Matthew's Gospel, when he speaks about a 'scribe trained for the kingdom of heaven bringing out of his treasure what is new and what is old' (Matt. 13: 52).

doctrine of [religious] freedom has roots in *divine revelation*' (*DH* 9; emphasis added).

When articles 2–8 expressed what 'centuries' of experience had made known, the declaration appealed to philosophical anthropology and insights into a constitutional order of society, based on justice and 'human dignity' (*DH* 3). 'Human dignity' formed the (Latin) title of the document and recurred in articles 2, 3, and 9. It was from the dignity of the human person created in the divine image (Gen. 1: 26–7) that John XXIII in his 1963 encyclical *Pacem in Terris* had drawn his extensive treatment of human rights which concerned such matters as life, education, and religious freedom (DzH 3956–72; ND 2026–42). This encyclical, cited four times in the footnotes attached to articles 2–8 of *Dignitatis Humanae*, provided a major witness supporting the case for civil authorities protecting the inviolable rights of citizens—in particular, the religious freedom and equality of all before the law. Yet papal teaching upholding the principle of religious freedom (*DH* 2–8) could be retrieved only as far back as Leo XIII.

Third, what obviously proved more powerfully significant was the theological appeal to the revelation mediated through Christ and his apostles (*DH* 9–15). In essence, the declaration argued that Jesus always respected human freedom and, specifically, the religious freedom of human beings. Their faith could not be and should not be coerced (*DH* 12). His disciples followed him by maintaining that the human response to God must be free, as well as by asserting their own right to proclaim the good news (*DH* 9–11).

As part of this biblical-theological defence of religious freedom, *Dignitatis Humanae* appealed to tradition in the form of teaching that comes from four fathers of the Church (Lactantius, Ambrose, Augustine, and Gregory the Great) and two medieval popes (Clement III and Innocent III). Here the declaration might also have referenced Pope Nicholas I (d. 867). In a letter sent to the ruler of Bulgaria, he rejected any violent means for forcing people to accept the Christian faith, which had just been officially accepted in the country (DzH 647–8).

But it was above all through retrieving the New Testament's witness to the practice and teaching of Jesus that *Dignitatis Humanae* set itself to correct distorted and false traditional teaching: in particular, the long-standing conviction that 'error has no rights'. A retrieval of Scripture, which also included the dignity of human beings created in the image and likeness of God (Gen. 1: 26–7), reversed nineteenth-century papal teaching and supported religious freedom in civil society.

Relations with Jews

This chapter has been written out of the conviction that an adequate understanding of the interplay between the fixed, canonical Scriptures and developing (and changing) traditions in the Christian Church can come only from examining concrete examples. Otherwise, we are doomed to use the insipid, shop-worn language of old slogans.

Where *Dignitatis Humanae*, under pressure from the Scriptures, brought an official 'about face' in official teaching on religious freedom, Vatican II's 1964 Dogmatic Constitution on the Church, *Lumen Gentium*, and 1965 Declaration on the Relation of the Church to Non-Christian Religions, *Nostra Aetate*, did the same in what was taught about Jews, Muslims, and others. I wish to focus here on the change in language about Jews.

Lumen Gentium proved the first time in Catholic Christianity that an ecumenical council had ever spoken well of the Jews or, for that matter, of Muslims.[26] In its 1442 decree for Copts, the Council of Florence declared: 'the holy Roman Church . . . firmly believes, professes, and preaches that no one remaining outside the Catholic Church, not only pagans, but also Jews, heretics, and schismatics can become partakers of eternal life, but they will go to the eternal fire prepared for the devil and his angels' (DzH 1351; ND 810). It would take a huge historical parenthesis to explain (but not justify) such negative teaching that was reflected in so many Catholic (and Christian) traditions. It took over five hundred years for this teaching to be reversed and then only after the Shoah, when Adolf Hitler (1889–1945) and his collaborators systematically exterminated nearly 6 million European Jews, 1 million of them children.

Lumen Gentium selected some of the privileges listed by Romans 9: 4–5 to speak of 'the people to whom the covenants and promises were given and from whom Christ was born according to the flesh'. Then it

[26] See G. O'Collins, *The Second Vatican Council: Message and Meaning* (Collegeville, MN: Liturgical Press, 2014), 109–11, 116, 197–202.

further aligned itself with Paul by stating that 'according to the [divine] election, they [the Jews] are a people most dear on account of the fathers; for the gifts and calling of God are without regret [*sine poenitentia*] (Rom. 11: 28–9)' (*LG* 16). Here Vatican II found its scriptural warrant (for changed teaching about the Jews) in the texts of Paul about God's irrevocable election of Israel—texts that no previous ecumenical council had cited or even referred to.[27]

In a longer reflection on the Jewish people that appeared a year later in *Nostra Aetate*, the Council once again quoted Romans 9: 4–5 (*NA* 4). In a reference to Romans 11: 28–9, it recalled the use of those verses in *Lumen Gentium* 16 (*NA* 4, n. 11). *Nostra Aetate*, with only five articles, is the shortest of all the sixteen documents promulgated by the Second Vatican Council. But more than half a century of post-conciliar history has seen it grow in theological and pastoral significance, and not least for its importance in Christian–Jewish dialogue and collaboration. Key chapters from Paul's Letter to the Romans played a central role in challenging and changing traditions tainted by anti-Semitism.[28]

Instead of straw men conjured up for the occasion, this chapter has taken up five examples that throw light on the interplay between Scripture and tradition: the emergence and function of classic creeds; the success of Paul's profiling Christ as the 'second' or 'last Adam'; the Reformation controversy over justification; the about face of Catholic teaching on religious freedom; and the impact of Romans 9 and 11 in challenging and changing attitudes towards the Jewish people.

---

[27] Rom. 9: 4–5 entered what would become the text of *LG*, thanks to the schema elaborated by Gérard Philips that, from February 1963, became the basis for a revised draft. After emendations were received, Rom. 11: 28–9 entered the text in 1964. See G. Alberigo and F. Magistretti (eds), *Constitutionis Dogmaticae Lumen Gentium Synopsis Historica* (Bologna: Istututo per le Scienze Religiose, 1975), 71.

[28] See J. M. Oesterreicher, 'Declaration on the Relation of the Church to Non-Christian Religions', in H. Vorgrimler (ed.), *Commentary on the Documents of Vatican II*, iii (London: Burns & Oates, 1969), 1–136; and P. A. Cunningham et al., 'The Road Behind and the Road Ahead: Catholicism and Judaism', in J. L. Heft (ed.), *Catholicism and Interreligious Dialogue* (New York: Oxford University Press, 2012), 23–56.

Chapter 4 of my *Inspiration: Towards a Christian Interpretation of Biblical Inspiration*[29] fills out the picture of how the Scriptures, both Old and New Testaments, have exercised an enduring and worldwide influence on Christian worship, preaching, official teaching, hymns, visual art, and daily life. The illuminating, corrective, and nourishing force of the inspired Scriptures on the tradition of Christians can be documented abundantly. The four volumes of *The New Cambridge History of the Bible*[30] provide the best commentary on the interplay between Scripture and tradition.

Beyond question, the authority of divine inspiration belongs to the Scriptures.[31] But they need to be read, interpreted, and applied by tradition. Concrete, historical examples enrich and even change the way we see the mutual dependence of Scripture and tradition.

---

[29] (Oxford: Oxford University Press, 2018).   [30] See n. 1 above.

[31] In his review of my *Revelation* (see n. 6 above), Mark Ord expressed his disappointment over not finding 'an articulation of inspiration that gave as much attention to narrative as to propositions' (70). I have now published much on narrative and metanarrative in *Inspiration: Towards a Christian Interpretation of Biblical Inspiration* (Oxford: Oxford University Press, 2018). In any case the distinction between 'narrative' and 'propositions' is less than perfect; narratives can contain many propositions.

6

Discerning Particular Traditions

In the early twenty-first century, few people would challenge the statement by Edward Shils: 'no society remains still. Each one is in unceasing change.'[1] He cites two triggers for change which, since he published *Tradition* in 1981, have increased exponentially, the revolution in communications and the movement of populations. 'Traditions change', he observes, 'when their adherents are brought or enter into the presence of other traditions'.[2] The presence of 'others' with their different cultural and religious traditions, such as Jews, Muslims, Hindus, Buddhists, and agnostics, have affected Catholics and other Christians everywhere. Recently in a city where fifty years ago Muslims could rarely be found, I celebrated the end of Ramadan with a group of imams and did so in the residence of the Catholic archbishop. The situation in which more and more people of diverse backgrounds live side by side has affected cultures and religions worldwide. Exposed to traditions of different sorts, believers have re-expressed and modified their beliefs and practices. Prior to the Second Vatican Council (1962–5), it would have been unthinkable in most countries for a Catholic bishop to host the local imams at a meal closing the month of Ramadan.

Traditions that Work or Fail to Work

Shils understands what is learned from *experience* to be decisive both in confirming and revising established traditions. On the one hand, 'a tradition has to work if it is to persist . . . A tradition which repeatedly

---

[1] E. Shils, *Tradition* (London: Faber and Faber, 1981), 163.
[2] Ibid. 240.

turns out to be obviously wrong will not persist.' On the other hand, traditions and beliefs 'which have been known to work are generally not lightly discarded'. Experience provides 'presumptive evidence' in their favour.[3] From innumerable examples we can cite cases that illustrate how Christian traditions work or, sooner or later, fail to work.

(1) Among examples of traditions that have worked and persisted, one can name teaching about 'the seven deadly sins', pilgrimages to Santiago de Compostela (and other shrines), the use of icons, and the Advent service of Nine Lessons and Carols. At first glance, this may appear an odd batch of examples, but let us see what they yield.

Considered to be the root of all other sins in a tradition developed by Evagrius Ponticus (d. 399) and Gregory the Great (d. 604), *the seven deadly sins* are pride, covetousness, lust, envy, gluttony, anger, and sloth. In his *Divine Comedy*, Dante Alighieri (d. 1321) gave a detailed account of the moral life by constructing a long climb up the mountain of purgatory and around seven terraces, on which sinners were cleansed from the seven deadly sins. These sins began with the worst (pride) and ended with the least serious sin of lust. Dante knew the biblical teaching of the Ten Commandments but judged that the doctrine of the seven deadly sins communicated better. For centuries his *Purgatorio* proved a vivid handbook for Christians examining their conscience about sins they had committed. Modern films, such as the 1962 French masterpiece *Les Sept péchés capitaux*, witness to the way in which the traditional doctrine of seven deadly (or capital) sins maintains its power and insight. Anyone who was fortunate enough to see the stage version of those sins expressed in silent mime by Marcel Marceau (d. 2007) will say the same. In modern times, the traditional teaching about seven deadly sins continues to work and will not be 'lightly discarded'.

By AD 250 the popular cult of Peter and Paul began to flourish in Rome and draw *pilgrims* to their tombs. After freedom came with the Emperor Constantine, pilgrimages to the Holy Land and to the tombs of Roman martyrs increased. In 326, Helena, the saintly mother of Constantine, went on pilgrimage to the Holy Land and founded

---

[3] Ibid. 203–4.

basilicas to enshrine the memory of Jesus' life, death, resurrection, and ascension. A work from the end of fourth century, the *Pilgrimage of Etheria*, provides reports from a Christian lady (probably a Spaniard) who visited Jerusalem and its neighbourhood. The tradition of pilgrimages to Rome, Palestine, and other homes to holy shrines has never ceased.[4] Dante used the pilgrimage theme right from the opening lines of the *Comedy*: 'in the middle of our life's journey I found myself in a dark wood—the way ahead lost' (trans. mine). The spiritual transformation of Dante the pilgrim takes him through hell and purgatory to heaven. In 'real' life, Dante himself went on pilgrimage to Rome in the jubilee year of 1300. Other ancient and modern places of Christian pilgrimage came to include Lough Derg (Ireland), Santiago de Compostela (Spain), and the Marian shrines of Aparecida (Brazil), Czestochowa (Poland), Fatima (Portugal), Guadalupe (Mexico), Lourdes (France), Walsingham (England), and the island of Tinos, where the Orthodox celebrate in a special way the 'dormition' (or falling asleep at the end of her life) of Our Lady.

The ancient Celts called such shrines 'thin places'; time and again they walked to some shrine and, at journey's end, experienced close communion with God. For many centuries, St Patrick's Purgatory on Station Island in Lough Derg (Donegal) has exercised its fascination and impact on generations of pilgrims. A Nobel laureate, Seamus Heaney (d. 2013), came several times and expressed his experiences in a sequence of poems, *Station Island*.

A 1995 novel by David Lodge, *Therapy*, catches the impact of pilgrimages to Santiago de Compostela. So too did the 2011 film *The Way* which starred Martin Sheen as a doctor who makes the *camino*, scatters the ashes of his dead son along the way, bonds in friendship with three other pilgrims, and finds some meaning in his terrible loss and grief. The film subtly conveys the personal transformation experienced through the pilgrimage. In 'Finding Forgiveness', James Jeffrey, who left the British army as a captain in 2010, tells how he eventually made a *camino* to confront 'the anger and guilt' he continued to feel over his period of service in Iraq and Afghanistan.

---

[4] See Diana Webb, *Pilgrims and Pilgrimages in the Medieval West* (London: Tauris, 1999).

Part of his job in Afghanistan 'involved helping to coordinate close air support for ground troops involved in firefights, which sometimes resulted in women and children being killed by bomb drops'. He made a confession near the cathedral of Santiago de Compostela, and as part of his penance was asked to seek 'the forgiveness of the men, women and children' whom he and his comrades had killed. 'It was the breakthrough', Jeffrey remarks, 'that had previously completely eluded me.' The *camino* and confession 'proved far more efficacious than all the advice and counselling' that he had received since he returned from the war in Afghanistan.[5]

Paul Connerton has written eloquently of the effective role of pilgrimages and other such traditional 'bodily practices' in transmitting and nurturing Christian faith.[6] The 'presumptive evidence' in favour of the practice of pilgrimages ensures the future of this tradition. A Christianity that would abandon the tradition of pilgrimages is unthinkable. Iona, a small island in the Inner Hebrides where St Columba built a church and monastery in the sixth century, and Walsingham (Norfolk), a medieval place of pilgrimage that has been restored, both show how Christians of different traditions (Anglicans, Catholics, and Protestants) can unite in pilgrimages that enhance and hand on their faith.[7]

As sacred images for public and private worship in Eastern churches, *icons* undoubtedly form a tradition that 'works' and has long ago spread widely in Western Christianity as well. Likewise, the service of *Nine Lessons and Carols*, introduced in 1880 by Bishop Edward White Benson (then Bishop of Truro and later Archbishop of Canterbury), has been adopted worldwide by many Christian churches. Icons and this service are two shining examples of traditions, one ancient and the other relatively modern, that belong

[5] J. Jeffrey, 'Finding Forgiveness', *The Tablet*, 23/30 December 2017, 27–8.

[6] P. Connerton, *How Societies Remember* (New York: Cambridge University Press, 1989), 72–104. He dedicates some pages to pilgrimages in his later book, *How Modernity Forgets* (New York: Cambridge University Press, 2009), 14–18.

[7] For details and bibliography, see F. L. Cross and E. A. Livingstone (eds), *The Oxford Dictionary of the Christian Church*, 3rd edn (Oxford: Oxford University Press, 2005), 848 ('Iona') and 1730 ('Walsingham').

to 'the living tradition of the whole Church' (*DV* 12).[8] While reading this phrase ecumenically and recognizing that the mutual enrichment of Christian churches goes beyond the explicit intentions of those who drafted and accepted Vatican II's Constitution on Divine Revelation, how else can we characterize the examples of icons and the service of Nine Lessons and Carols? Like so much else—including supremely the practice of baptism in the name of the Trinity—they form an unchallenged part of the living and life-giving tradition for innumerable, if not all, Christians and will not 'turn out to be obviously wrong'.

(2) In the last chapter we examined in detail two traditions which eventually were officially declared wrong by the Second Vatican Council: the denial of religious freedom and the evil of anti-Semitism, which for centuries showed up in a Good Friday prayer about 'the perfidious Jews'.

The refusal of the sacraments to divorced Catholics who are civilly remarried would now, in the light of the 2016 apostolic exhortation of Pope Francis, *Amoris Laetitia* (the Joy of Love),[9] seem to be another case of a tradition that does not work. For a long time, the sacraments were not available for such couples, unless they took 'on themselves the duty to live in complete continence, that is, by abstinence from the acts proper to married couple'.[10] A 1981 exhortation on the Christian family by Pope John Paul II, *Familiaris Consortio* (*FC*), called this teaching a church 'practice [*consuetudinem*]'—not a defined doctrine, yet one based on the Sacred Scriptures, even if he did not quote any particular biblical passages. He stated that 'the state and condition of life' of such divorced and remarried couples 'objectively contradict that union of love between Christ and the Church which is signified and effected by the Eucharist' (*FC* 84). This obviously referred to Ephesians 5: 22–33, where the union of married couples is compared

---

[8] The phrase occurs in a chapter on the inspiration and interpretation of Sacred Scriptures (*DV* 11–13).

[9] Pope Francis, *Amoris Laetitia* (Vatican City: Libreria Editrice Vaticana, 2016); hereafter *AL*.

[10] Pope John Paul II, homily at the close of the Sixth Synod of Bishops (25 October 1980), 7; *Acta Apostolicae Sedis* 72 (1980), 1082; these words are quoted by *FC* 84.

to that between Christ and the Church.[11] But neither the Pauline teaching nor, for that matter, any other biblical passage invoke *the Eucharist as signifying and effecting* the loving union between Christ and the Church, the union of married couples, and the link between these two unions. John Paul II had dedicated earlier articles in *Familiaris Consortio* to Christ the bridegroom of the Church and the sacrament of matrimony (*FC* 13) and to the Eucharistic dimension of the community of life and love which is marriage (*FC* 57).[12] Article 57 speaks of Christian marriage being 'intimately connected to' and 'continuously renewed' by the Eucharist. Here we find the immediate background to the language of article 84 about the Eucharist signifying and effecting a union of love.

John Paul II added a further, pastoral reason for continuing to refuse the Eucharist to the divorced in a second (civil) marriage: 'if these people were admitted to the Eucharist, the faithful would be led into error and confusion regarding the Church's teaching about the indissolubility of marriage' (*FC* 84). This ecclesial teaching rests, of course, on what Jesus said about marriage and against remarriage, but *Familiaris Consortio* makes only a limited reference to the Lord's words on this issue (*FC* 10, 13).[13] The exhortation recognizes that those in second marriage may have 'serious reasons' for not separating: for instance, 'the children's upbringing'. It asks, nevertheless, that they live 'in complete continence' or, in frequently used terminology, as brother and sister. If they do so, they can be reconciled through the sacrament of penance and receive Holy Communion (*FC* 84). Here one cannot help asking whether other Catholics who then see such couples receiving Communion will not be 'led into error and confusion' about the Church's teaching on the indissolubility of marriage. Or have they a right to know that these divorced and remarried

[11] *FC* 13, when comparing the marriage union and the union of Christ with the Church, evidently meant to refer to Eph. 5: 22–33 (fn. 28), but mistakenly cites 5: 32–3; see *Acta Apostolicae Sedis* 74 (1982), 82–191, at 94.

[12] In his 2007 exhortation on the Eucharist, *Sacramentum Caritatis* (Vatican City: Libreria Editrice Vaticana, 2007), Pope Benedict XVI remarked that 'Pope John Paul II frequently spoke of the nuptial character of the Eucharist and its special relationship with the sacrament of matrimony' (art. 27).

[13] For the teaching of Jesus against divorce and remarriage, see J. P. Meier, *A Marginal Jew*, iv (New Haven, CT: Yale University Press, 2009), 74–81.

couples are now living 'in complete continence'? Have such couples the obligation of disclosing (e.g. to the members of their parish) the change in their mutual relationship? Or has their parish priest who now gives these couples Holy Communion the duty of explaining to 'the faithful' what has happened to justify his no longer refusing the sacrament to those who are divorced and civilly remarried?

Despite the teaching of *Familiaris Consortio*, three German bishops, Oskar Seiler and (the future cardinals) Karl Lehmann and Walter Kasper, subsequently issued a pastoral letter (dated 10 July 1993) proposing that the divorced and remarried who were sexually active could, under appropriate circumstances, receive Holy Communion. This pastoral solution to a very real problem was rejected by Pope John Paul II and Cardinal Joseph Ratzinger.[14] But in *Amoris Laetitia*, Pope Francis retrieved the teaching of Lehmann, Kasper, and Seiler and cited the traditional solution about living as brother and sister maintained by *Familiaris Consortio*, but would not endorse that solution. He quoted Vatican II's Constitution on the Church in the Modern World to observe that, 'if certain expressions of intimacy are lacking, it often happens that faithfulness is endangered and the good of the children suffers' (*AL* 298, fn. 329; see *GS* 51). Pastoral experience trumps other considerations and sets aside a traditional teaching on marriage that is now seen not to work. We will return below to the case of *Amoris Laetitia*. Here it is invoked to fill out the vision of inherited traditions that we can sort out as working or failing to work.

Shared Pastoral Experience

The oldest extant Christian document, The First Letter of Paul to the Thessalonians, witnesses to the need for discernment: 'Do not quench the Spirit. Do not despise the words of prophets, but test everything. Hold fast to what is good; abstain from every form of evil' (1 Thess. 5: 19–22). Those gifted with prophecy should be heard; refusing to do so would be trying to curb the possibility of Spirit-inspired help. Nevertheless, everything is to be tested and only what is 'good' should be

[14] The three German bishops wrote: 'it ought to be clarified through pastoral dialogue whether that which is generally valid applies also to a given situation': *Origins* 23/38 (10 March 1994), 670–6, at 673.

accepted and followed in practice. The First Letter of John likewise calls for the testing of 'spirits' to ensure that they truly come from God (1 John 4: 1–6). It presents this testing in terms of questions about Jesus Christ and the Holy Spirit ('the Spirit of truth'). We will return to these questions below.

Living nearly two thousand years later than Paul and John, contemporary Christians and their leaders have inherited numerous beliefs and patterns of action. They may accept such traditions, modify them, or even reject them. But how should they go about the task of testing their patrimony? What counts as appropriate reasons for endorsing, renewing, or rejecting this or that tradition? What will allow the Christian community to embrace and live more fully all that is true, good, and beautiful in the good news of Jesus Christ? Some traditional elements in contemporary Christianity may fail to represent the full reality of the Gospel; some proposed changes may misrepresent the Gospel.

A philosopher friend of mine describes truth as 'that which is capable of yielding evidence upon investigation'. Rather than indulge a huge parenthesis to discuss his vision of truth, I want to try it out by proposing some sources and procedures that upon investigation seem to offer relevant evidence for the truth about inherited traditions.

Data that could be significant in discerning existing traditions comes from present, *shared pastoral experience*. In speaking of 'pastoral experience', I have in mind (a) what applies to numerous worshipping and practising Christians and not (b) what is confined to a single individual. In the passages quoted above from Paul and John, they both ask communities of Christians to deliberate in common or 'test' (plural) what they have experienced. It will be group discernment that should be guided by the Holy Spirit, which will yield the needed evidence and enable them to recognize the action of God in the traditions they have experienced.

(a) In *Prayer and the Priesthood of Christ in the Reformed Tradition*,[15] Graham Redding observes that traditions of liturgical leadership which do not include a vivid sense of Christ's mediatorial priesthood become theologically impoverished and move towards a personality

---

[15] (London: T. & T. Clark, 2003), 296–9.

cult of 'the so-called worship leader'. Rich pastoral experience, acquired and evaluated with many others, encouraged another Reformed theologian, the late Tom Torrance, to endorse a similar liturgical tradition of Christ's high priesthood, built upon the Letter to the Hebrews and the Christological teaching of the ancient Church.[16]

Pastoral experience and practice, and not simply theological and historical research, underpinned the modern liturgical movement that began in the nineteenth century and has encouraged among Christians the tradition of celebrating more frequently the Eucharist and the sense that the Eucharist is 'received as a gift from Christ living in the Church'. What many Christians experience at Eucharistic worship gives credibility to the way in which a Faith and Order paper of the World Council of Churches describes the renewed tradition of this supreme 'gift from Christ': 'In the celebration of the Eucharist, Christ gathers, teaches, and nourishes the Church. It is Christ who invites to the meal and who presides at it. He is the shepherd who leads the people of God, the prophet who announces the Word of God, the priest who celebrates the mystery of God.'[17]

Shared pastoral experience prompted many reforms of liturgical traditions proposed by Vatican II's Constitution on the Sacred Liturgy: for instance, eliminating 'useless repetitions' (*SC* 34; see 50), restoring more varied and suitable readings from the Scriptures (*SC* 35; see 51), and introducing the wider use of the vernacular (*SC* 36; see 54). Long-standing pastoral experience supported the Constitution's conviction that in the Western Church the traditional rites for administering the sacraments had become 'far from clear to the people of today'. The rites all needed to be revised to convey more effectively the nature and purpose of the sacraments (*SC* 62–78).

(b) Sometimes judgements about traditions and, in particular, liturgical traditions, are made on an individual basis that fails to include shared, pastoral experience. From the 1960s I recall one priest, a

[16] On Torrance, see G. O'Collins and M. K. Jones, *Jesus Our Priest: A Christian Approach to the Priesthood of Christ* (Oxford: Oxford University Press, 2010), 224–9.

[17] *Baptism, Eucharist and Ministry*, Faith and Order Paper No. 111 (Geneva: World Council of Churches, 1982), 16; hereafter *BEM*. Note the appeal to Christ's triple redemptive function: as shepherd/king, prophet, and priest, even if the passage does not adopt the usual sequence of priest, prophet, shepherd/king.

former artillery major in the British army, reluctantly agreeing to celebrate the Eucharist with the altar facing the people and remarking: 'I don't like the change. But orders are orders.' He had little interest in reflecting with others on the effect of this change in implementing a major pastoral aim of Vatican II, the full and active participation of the people in celebrating the liturgy. Even less did he want to be reminded that this change retrieved an ancient tradition, the liturgical practice of the early Church.

Much more recently a layman told me how disturbed he was by 'women invading the sanctuary'. He had joined a group to recite the rosary in a parish church, and was shocked by a woman going into the sanctuary and facing the congregation to lead them in prayer. He did not seem to notice that the others present took for granted what happened. I shared with him experiences from around the world: a young woman entering the sanctuary to read the first lesson at Mass in St Peter's Basilica (Rome); a Filipino woman in Westminster Cathedral (London) taking the arm of an aged canon, leading him from the altar down some steps, and then distributing Holy Communion with him; women cantors in many churches in the United States; on Good Friday an English actress expertly 'narrating' from a pulpit in Wimbledon the passion according St John; and a Chinese altar girl in a Melbourne church which I regularly attend on Sundays. She carries the thurible and, with graceful dignity, incenses at the appropriate times the celebrant, the other ministers, and the congregation. On these and so many other occasions, I have noticed how the people present happily accept women sharing in these ministries, especially when they do so with reverent expertise. Of course, women 'invading the sanctuary' in these ways represents a major change in the liturgical tradition of the (Western) Catholic Church. But pastoral experience around the world supports this reform. I hope the liturgy will be further renewed by a decision to ordain women deacons; that could follow the findings of a special commission established by Pope Francis to examine the matter.[18]

---

[18] In 2002 the International Theological Commission produced a document, *Le Diaconat: Évolution et perspectives*, which, though somewhat unsatisfactory, left open the ordination of women to the diaconate; see G. O'Collins, *Living Vatican II: The 21st Council for the 21st Century* (Mahwah, NJ: Paulist Press, 2006), 163–5.

Old Testament examples of challenges addressed to the people by Jeremiah and other prophets warn us, to be sure, against presuming that the community rather than some individual is always the repository of truth. Nevertheless, Paul and John (see above) advise the practice of discernment taking place in common rather than on an individual basis. One can readily find sad examples of the harm done when individuals override the decisions of groups of Christians—even national conferences of bishops. This happened when a handful of Vatican authorities peremptorily put aside, even without any collegial discussion, a translation of the liturgy that had already been approved by all eleven English-speaking conferences of Catholic bishops: the 1998 Missal.[19]

Apostolic Tradition Guiding Discernment

Besides common discernment of contemporary pastoral experience, evaluation of Christian traditions requires reflection on the past: both the inspired record of the Church's prophetic and apostolic foundations and the history of post-New Testament Christianity. *Biblical traditions* and *post-New Testament traditions* throw light on current traditions and may suggest their modification and even abolition.

The previous chapter recalled examples from the Second Vatican Council where reflection on biblical texts supported such changes in long-standing traditions as a clear endorsement of religious freedom and a firm condemnation of anti-Semitism. We could take up other examples, like the teaching on the collegial authority of the bishops (*LG* 22–4). The term 'collegiality' was new to Vatican II, but its New Testament background is to be found in the 'college' of apostles led by St Peter. Through their episcopal ordination and through being in communion with the head of the college (the bishop of Rome) and other bishops, new bishops become members of a worldwide college. This reclaimed, apostolic tradition of episcopal collegiality has been expressed in formal meetings: notably, through national and international conferences and through the episcopal synods which have

---

[19] See G. O'Collins and J. Wilkins, *Lost in Translation: The English Language and the Catholic Mass* (Collegeville, MN: Liturgical Press, 2017).

met regularly in Rome since 1967. In both cases many bishops, including the current bishop of Rome, Pope Francis, and other Catholics would like to see the tradition of episcopal collegiality more strongly encouraged and endorsed.[20]

To examine thoroughly traditions that were renewed, modified, or abandoned by the Second Vatican Council would require a book-length study.[21] The examples I have already cited show the Council concerned to maintain and renew the traditions of what Blessed John Henry Newman called 'the very religion which Christ and his apostles taught in the first' century.[22] This is the equivalent of maintaining and renewing *the apostolic identity* of the Church and the traditions in which it is embodied and through which it lives.[23] A similar deep concern shines through the teaching on baptism, Eucharist, and ministry produced by the Faith and Order Commission of the World Council of Churches.[24] The authors of *BEM* aimed at nothing less than retrieving and rejuvenating apostolic traditions that affect the meaning and practice of baptism, the nature and celebration of the Eucharist, and the role of ordained ministry in the life of the Church.

A renewed search for apostolicity and traditions that express it touches three areas: (a) the faith and theological insights of the apostolic Church, (b) the sacramental and organizational structures of the foundational Christian communities, and (c) the caring relationships for those in need manifested, for instance, by the collection sponsored by Paul on behalf of the poor Christians of Jerusalem.[25] Let me give examples illustrating the three areas.

---

[20] See G. O'Collins and M. Farrugia, *Catholicism: The Story of Catholic Christianity*, 2nd edn (Oxford: Oxford University Press, 2015), 408–11. For Vatican II's teaching on the collegial authority of bishops, see G. O'Collins, *The Second Vatican Council: Message and Meaning* (Collegeville, MN: Liturgical Press, 2014), 192–6.

[21] See O'Collins, *The Second Vatican Council*, 25–56.

[22] J. H. Newman, *An Essay on the Development of Christian Doctrine* (New York: Doubleday, 1960), 33.

[23] On the apostolic character and identity of the Church, see Lutheran–Roman Catholic Commission on Unity, *The Apostolicity of the Church* (Minneapolis: Lutheran University Press, 2006).

[24] See fn. 17 above.

[25] *BEM* expounds apostolic tradition as 'continuity in the permanent characteristics of the Church of the apostles: witness to the apostolic faith, proclamation

(a) The New Testament pervasively witnesses to the apostolic faith that all the baptized are called to true holiness (e.g. 2 Cor. 1: 1; 1 Thess. 4: 3; 1 Pet. 1: 16). Vatican II aimed at bringing back this tradition—not least through the chapter dedicated to the universal call to live genuinely holy lives (*LG* 39–42).

(b) As part of what *BEM* named 'the transmission of ministerial responsibilities', the Council prescribed returning to the ancient tradition of ordaining permanent deacons—that is to say, deacons who would continue to serve as such and not move on to priestly ordination (*LG* 29).

(c) *BEM* also listed under apostolic tradition 'service to the sick and needy' and 'sharing the gifts' given by the Lord. Vatican II's Constitution on the Church in the Modern World wrote large this caring relationship to all human beings by its teaching on 'the common good', 'respect for the human person', 'social justice', and 'human solidarity' (*GS* 26–32), 'economic development in the service of human beings' (*GS* 64), 'international action to prevent war' (*GS* 82), and much else besides. Clear reference to the apostolic tradition in the form of Christ's teaching (Matthew 25: 31–46; Luke 16: 19–31) underwrote the Council's renewed commitment to care for all those in need (*GS* 27).

Post-New Testament Developments

Many debates about specific traditions involve post-New Testament developments: for instance, the English translation of the Nicene Creed. The original Greek verb (*pisteuomen*) with which the Creed opened should have been translated into Latin as '*credimus* [we believe]' but was frequently (but by no means always) rendered in the singular as '*credo* [I believe]'. If we continue the tradition of speaking of the Nicene Creed (or, more accurately, of the

---

and fresh interpretation of the Gospel, celebration of baptism and the Eucharist, the transmission of ministerial responsibilities, communion in prayer, love, joy, and suffering, service to the sick and needy, unity among the local churches, and sharing the gifts which the Lord has given to each' (28). This list corresponds to my three areas, specifying further details in each of the areas.

Nicene-Constantinopolitan Creed), we should be true to the text of AD 381 and say 'we believe'.[26]

At times special commissions have been tasked with reflecting (in the light of the Scriptures and post-New Testament history) on traditions that have come under scrutiny and challenge: for instance, rejection of contraception and of the ordination of women to the ministerial priesthood. At the request of Paul VI, the question of methods of birth control was left to a commission of experts first appointed in 1964 by the Pope himself (*GS* 51, n. 14). A clear majority on the commission came out in favour of a change in traditional teaching. After prayerfully examining their report and consulting with others, Paul VI published in 1968 his encyclical *Humanae Vitae* ('Of Human Life'). While recognizing the importance of married love and endorsing responsible parenthood, the Pope continued the tradition of rejecting contraception. He appealed to the inseparable connection between the unitive and procreative meaning of sexual intercourse, and declared that 'each and every married act' must be open to the transmission of life (art. 11). Although an authoritative statement, the encyclical never claimed to be infallible teaching. The bishops of many countries invoked mitigating circumstances in its interpretation. The French bishops, for instance, would not unconditionally exclude artificial means of birth control, which they considered 'a lesser evil' when periodical continence proves impossible or when spouses are faced with a conflict of duties.[27]

In the 1970s the Pontifical Biblical Commission was entrusted with examining the tradition of limiting priestly ordination to men and excluding women. In its final report the Commission unanimously concluded: 'It does not seem that the New Testament by itself alone will permit us to settle in a clear way and once and for all the problem

---

[26] See O'Collins and Wilkins, *Lost in Translation*, 28–9, 42.

[27] On the tradition of opposition to contraception, see John T. Noonan, *Contraception: A History of its Treatment by Catholic Theologians and Canonists* (Cambridge, MA: Belknap Press of Harvard University Press, 1986). On the birth control commission, see Robert Blair Kaiser, *The Encyclical That Never Was: The Story of the Pontifical Commission on Population, Family and Birth, 1964–66* (London: Sheed & Ward, 1987); for the final report of the Commission, see ibid. 3–18.

of the possible accession of women to the presbyterate.'[28] Nevertheless, at its April 1976 meeting the Commission voted twelve to seven
that it would not seem to go against 'Christ's original intentions', if
women were to be entrusted with 'the ministries of eucharist and
reconciliation'.[29]

In a declaration dated 15 October 1976 but published on
27 January 1977, *Inter Insigniores*, the Congregation for the Doctrine
of the Faith (CDF) rejected admitting women to the priestly ministry:
'The Church, in fidelity to the example of the Lord, does not consider
itself authorized to admit women to priestly ordination.' The CDF
gave six reasons for this response:

> 1) The Church's constant tradition has been to ordain only men to the
> priestly ministry; 2) Jesus did not call any women to be members of the
> Twelve; 3) the apostles did not include any women in the apostolic
> group; 4) the practice of Christ and the apostles in this regard is
> permanently normative; 5) the priest must have a 'natural resemblance'
> to Christ, and the male sex is constitutive of this resemblance; 6) the
> issue of equality in the Church and of human rights is irrelevant to the
> question of priestly ministry for women.   (ND 749–51)[30]

Inter Insigniores included no reference to the very recent report of the
Pontifical Biblical Commission—an omission made even more striking
by the fact that the prefect of the CDF was also *ex officio* president of the
Commission. The key question for the CDF was: Can such a constant
tradition be changed? Compared with the report of the Biblical Commission, *Inter Insigniores* looks notably weak when commenting on the
New Testament witness. Apropos of the second reason adduced by the
CDF, for instance, many have remarked that Jesus did not call any
non-Jews to be members of the Twelve. But that did not stand in the
way of his Church including innumerable Gentiles among its leaders
and not merely among its members. The first reason (the Church may
not change such a constant tradition) remains the key issue.

---

[28] Arlene Swidler and Leonard Swidler (eds), *Women Priests* (New York: Paulist
Press, 1977), 338–46, at 346.

[29] Ibid. 25, 346.

[30] For the full text, see *Acta Apostolicae Sedis* 69 (1977), 98–116; Swidler and
Swidler, *Women Priests* supplies an English translation, 37–49.

Learning from Others

When engaged in testing and discerning traditions they have inherited, Roman Catholics can learn from their fellow Christians, other religious faiths and cultures, and the secular world. Let us take up in turn these three groups.

(1) In its Constitution on the Church, the Second Vatican Council recognized the 'many elements of sanctification and truth', 'gifts' from God that are found among other Christian churches that are not, or are not yet, in full union with the Catholic Church (*LG* 8). The Constitution pressed on to list some of the major graces Catholics share with those who are not in communion with the Bishop of Rome: baptism, faith in the Trinity, and the role of the Scriptures lead the list (*LG* 15). The Decree on Ecumenism (*Unitatis Redintegratio*) spelt out principles and hopes for ecumenical dialogues, which have emerged as part of mainstream Christianity. Such dialogues are two-way streets, with both sides learning as well as sharing. Moving beyond Vatican II's language of 'separated brethren', Pope Francis has written of fellow 'pilgrims journeying alongside each other'. 'We can learn so much from one another! It is not just about being better informed about others, but rather of reaping what the Spirit has sown in them, which is also meant to be a gift for us.' He offers the example of Catholics learning more from their Orthodox brothers and sisters 'about the meaning of episcopal collegiality and their experience of synodality'.[31] This papal advice should impel those Catholics who are engaged, officially or unofficially, with discerning traditions of collegiality and synodality to take on board what the Orthodox have experienced in these two areas.

This book has drawn attention to what might be learned from two Faith and Order documents: the 1963 Montreal report on tradition (Chapter 1), and the 1982 *BEM* paper on baptism, the Eucharist, and ministry (this chapter). Now classic texts, these two carefully nuanced documents offer much for any Christians bent on thinking about the traditions we have all inherited. Furthermore, we may not step aside from acknowledging what other Christians have contributed in many areas to current traditions of the Roman Catholic Church. This

---

[31] *Evangelii Gaudium* (Vatican City: Libreria Editrice Vaticana, 2013), 244, 246.

chapter has already mentioned the service of Nine Lessons and Carols. Innumerable Anglican and Protestant hymns have also come to enrich the musical tradition of the Catholic Church. The Catholics responsible for borrowing and adding these hymns to their musical heritage have recognized the truth and value that make the hymns suitable for worship. Catholic traditions of biblical scholarship have been improved by the best of Anglican and Protestant learning. In many changing areas of tradition, one can echo and extend what Pope Francis has written: we have learned so much from one another. Perhaps the most remarkable example comes from the Second Vatican Council itself. The Anglican, Orthodox, and Protestant observers did not as such have voting rights. But their influence on the discerning and drafting of texts that ushered in wide changes in Catholic traditions should not be underestimated. The Council records clearly and specifically support the observation of Pope Francis about learning from other Christians.[32]

Could it be that in the long run the Catholic Church will learn, for example, from the changed practice of the Anglican Communion (and other churches) and discern that ordaining women to the priestly ministry is a desirable change in an age-old tradition? It would be a serious mistake to confine to the past the possibility of Catholics learning from other Christians in the matter of discerning tradition.

(2) From its first document, the Constitution on the Sacred Liturgy (1963), to the final document it approved, the Constitution on the Church in the Modern World (1965), Vatican II showed itself ready to assimilate into the changes it was initiating 'the gifts and talents of

---

[32] W. M. Abbott and J. Gallagher (eds), *The Documents of Vatican II* (New York: Guild Press, 1966), includes comments on the documents by sixteen Protestant and Orthodox scholars and church leaders, some of whom (Robert McAfee Brown, Fred Pierce Corson, Frederick C. Grant, Albert C. Outler, and Warren A. Quanbeck) had been observers at the Council. On the contribution of the observers, see M. Velati, *Dialogo e rinnovamento: verbali e testi del segretariato per l'unità dei cristiani nella preparazione del Concilio Vaticano II, 1960–1962* (Bologna: Il Mulino, 2011); M. Velati, *Separati ma fratelli: Gli osservatori non-Cattolici al Vaticano II (1962–1965)* (Bologna: Il Mulino, 2014). For a list of non-Catholic delegates and guests and the sessions of Vatican II they attended, see A. Melloni (ed.), *Vatican II: The Complete History* (Mahwah, NJ: Paulist Press, 2015), 278.

various races and peoples' (*SC* 37). This meant that, after wise discernment, 'elements from the traditions and nature of individual peoples'
could be incorporated into divine worship (*SC* 40). The Council offered
an example: the traditional music of different peoples and cultures
(*SC* 119). The Decree on the Church's Missionary Activity acknowledged the elements of goodness found in 'the special rites and cultures
of peoples', which, so far from being lost, should be 'healed, raised to a
higher level, and brought to perfection' (*AG* 9, see 11). The same decree
constructs a vision of 'the young churches' that 'are rooted in Christ and
built on the foundation of the apostles': 'they borrow from the customs
and traditions, wisdom and teaching, arts and sciences of their peoples
everything that can contribute to confessing the glory of the Creator,
manifesting the grace of the Saviour, or rightly ordering Christian life'
(*AG* 22; see *LG* 13).

In its closing vision of fruitful dialogue with all groups of human
beings, Vatican II includes all those who acknowledge God and 'in
their traditions preserve precious religious and human elements'. The
Council hopes that dialogue with them 'will bring us all to receive the
impulses of the Spirit with fidelity and eagerly act upon them' (*GS* 92).
This appreciation of dialogue with followers of other religions both
recognizes 'precious religious elements in their traditions' and expects
'impulses of the Spirit' to be conveyed through the dialogue. In short,
Catholics and other Christians should not only share with the 'others'
but also learn from them—for instance, in the task of testing and
discerning traditions. What this could involve concretely has already
been sketched by earlier conciliar documents, notably *Ad Gentes* and
Sacrosanctum Concilium (see above).

The 1963 Montreal report of the Faith and Order Commission also
faced the situation of the Christian tradition being proclaimed in
'different lands and cultures' and meeting cultural diversity. The
Church, it was convinced, should 'become truly indigenous, bringing
into the service of Christ all that is good in the life of every culture and
nation, without falling into syncretism'. When 'the Church takes the
Tradition (*Christus praesens*) to new peoples, it is necessary that the
essential content should find expression in terms of new cultures'.[33]

---

[33] *Montreal 63*, 57–8.

Wise discernment obviously has to pull its weight in fashioning such new expressions through dialogue with other cultures and religions.

(3) Christians bent on scrutinizing, renewing, and reforming their traditions do well to let themselves be open to learning from the secular world. No longer governed by religious traditions and certainties, a secular, agnostic culture can, nevertheless, teach Christians or at least remind them of foundational beliefs that have been sidelined and ignored. In an article dedicated to 'what the Church receives from the modern world', the Second Vatican Council spoke of 'being helped by the Holy Spirit in listening to, discerning and distinguishing the various voices of our time', 'judging them in the light of the divine Word, in order that the revealed truth may be more deeply perceived, better understood, and more suitably presented'. But the article went further by acknowledging that 'the Church has been helped and can still be helped by the opposition of those who oppose her or even persecute her' (*GS* 44). The Constitution on the Church in the Modern World offers no instances of the Church benefiting from hostile and non-believing outsiders. Nevertheless, the criticisms of such outsiders played some role in the discernment that guided dropping opposition to religious freedom and producing the *Dignitatis Humanae*. Such outsiders prodded Christian bishops and theologians into retrieving part of the foundational tradition of the Church: the respect for the religious freedom of others shown by Christ and his apostles (see Chapter 5 above).

A readiness to learn from non-believers in matters of discerning Christian traditions follows from what *Lumen Gentium* teaches about morally upright atheists: 'whatever *good or truth* is found among them is considered by the Church to be a preparation for the Gospel, and given by him [the incarnate Word] who enlightens all human beings so that they may at length have life' (*LG* 16; emphasis added). This implies that, through the lives and words of such atheists and agnostics, a Christian could identify elements of goodness and truth, given by Christ the Light of the world. Hence, even if they lack awareness of its source in the living Christ, these outsiders can share truth with Christians: for instance, the truth of the right of human beings to enjoy religious liberty in civil society. Many of the details about respect for human dignity (*GS* 27) would be endorsed by upright non-believers and have in fact been promoted by them. The same is true of Vatican

II's teaching on social justice and the basic rights of all human beings (*GS* 29). When at this point of history Catholics and other Christians involve themselves in discerning such matters, it is at their peril that they fail to hear the voices of such non-believers.

The encyclical letter on ecology and climate, *Laudato Si'*, of Pope Francis, illustrates how Christian discernment can be helped and even guided also by the findings of non-believers.[34] Themes concerned with questions of ecology and climate were neglected by the Second Vatican Council, but have become ever more pressing since it closed in 1965. In his encyclical, Pope Francis drew on some elements of Christian tradition, for instance, the teaching and example of St Francis of Assisi (art. 10–12) and on teaching coming from sixteen bishops' conferences, and set himself to create a platform for a strong, new doctrine of care for our earth. In doing so he *also* drew on scientific studies (e.g. about the availability of water (art. 27–31)). He could even use studies provided right there in Rome by the Food and Agriculture Organization (e.g. art. 31, fn. 33) and the Pontifical Academy of Sciences (e.g. art. 131, fn. 110). The members not only of FAO but also of this academy are not necessarily Christians or even followers of other religious faiths. Yet their research on such matters as pollution, widespread soil degradation, and climate change obviously helped shape the renewed tradition launched by Pope Francis. This encyclical offers a striking example of how the discernment and renewal of Christian traditions may also learn from secular, non-believing sources.

In my own country (Australia), Christians and others responsible for discerning public policies need to hear such voices as those of Charles Massy.[35] Unless farmers, governments, and the general community turn against industrial methods of working the land and foster healthy ecosystems that respect nature, agriculture will be doomed. In Australia we must stop asking, 'What can we get out of the country?', and start asking, 'What can we do for the country?'

[34] Pope Francis, *Laudato Si': On Care for Our Common Home* (Vatican City: Libreria Editrice Vaticana, 2015).
[35] *Call of the Reed Warbler: A New Agriculture, A New Earth* (Brisbane: University of Queensland Press, 2017).

Retrieving the Wisdom and Practice of the Past

To complete this account of what can properly enter the process of discerning current Christian traditions, we need to add the retrieval of *forgotten traditions*. Chapter 4 has already mentioned a striking and successful example of such retrieval, the return that Vatican II mandated to catechumenate expressed in the Rite of Christian Initiation of Adults. This present chapter has cited above the recent case of Pope Francis changing a current tradition by discerning that access to Holy Communion should not be simply denied to Catholics who have been divorced and remarried civilly and do not agree (or cannot agree) to live as 'brother and sister' with their partner. After responsible reflection involving their parish priest and others, they may receive the sacraments of reconciliation and the Eucharist (*Amoris Laetitia*, 296–312).

In building his case for change, Pope Francis retrieves teaching from fathers of the Church and St Thomas Aquinas. He points out that the Eucharist is 'not a prize for the perfect but a powerful medicine and nourishment for the weak' (*AL* 305, fn. 351). This insight into the 'medicinal' and 'nourishing' power of the Eucharist goes back to the teaching of St Ignatius of Antioch about 'the one bread which is the medicine of immortality',[36] and to early liturgical prayers about the healing effected by the Eucharist.[37] In his apostolic exhortation *Evangelii Gaudium*, the Pope had already cited what St Ambrose of Milan and St Cyril of Alexandria taught about receiving the Eucharist for the forgiveness of sin.[38] A key theological argument

---

[36] *Epistle to the Ephesians*, 20.2; trans. M. Staniforth, *Early Christian Writings: The Apostolic Fathers* (London: Penguin, 1968), 82.

[37] An old post-Communion prayer for Monday of the Second Week of Lent (incorporated in the 1570 Missal of Pius V and in the 1970 Missal of Paul VI) asks that the Holy Communion in which we have just shared 'cleanse [us] from [our] offence [*purget a crimine*]'. Another old post-Communion prayer, that for Tuesday of the Fourth Week of Lent (found in the 1570 Missal of Pius V but not in the 1970 Missal of Paul VI) asks that 'the reception of this Sacrament, Lord, may purify us from [our] offence [*huius nos, Domine, perceptio sacramenti mundet a crimine*]'; trans. mine.

[38] *Evangelii Gaudium* (Vatican City: Libreria Editrice Vaticana, 2013), art. 47, n. 51.

for allowing access to the Eucharist of the divorced and civilly remarried is taken from ancient Christian teaching about the forgiving, healing, and nourishing power of the Eucharist.

An important passage in *Amoris Laetitia* also engages in retrieval by taking up the teaching of St Thomas Aquinas on the distinction between specific circumstances and 'general rules' that 'set forth a good which can never be disregarded or neglected'. In 'their formulation they [the rules] cannot provide absolutely for all particular situations' (art. 304).[39] The clarity that belongs to general principles (e.g. about marriage being exclusive and permanent) may not be found when we move to the details and complexities of particular cases.

Four Questions

Four questions can pull together much that should guide those who reflect on existing traditions and ensure that the good news of Christ remains living and effective in our world. First, what does prayerful pondering of the Scriptures say about maintaining or reforming particular traditions? Second, does this or that tradition contribute to the faithful being led more clearly by the Holy Spirit? Third, do these particular traditions help them worship more consciously with Christ the High Priest and set them closer to him in their life? Fourth, what traditions or what changed traditions will prompt them into serving more generously the needy and suffering?

The first question relates the task of discerning traditions to the Bible, the normative, written witness to the foundational revelation which created the Christian community. In the present period of dependent revelation, the Scriptures must continue to challenge, guide, and nourish the Church and every aspect of Christian life. There is no alternative to closely focusing on the Scriptures when evaluating particular traditions. We have seen the conclusion that Second Vatican Council reached when it brought the Word of God to bear on long-standing traditions that involved anti-Semitism and the denial of religious freedom.

---

[39] Thomas Aquinas, *Summa Theologiae*, I–II, q. 94, art. 4.

The second question relates the work of discernment to the experience of growing through the Holy Spirit more richly into the life of God (e.g. Rom. 8: 12–17). Do some inherited traditions allow believers to experience more deeply what Christ has brought them through the Spirit: the forgiveness of sins, the new life of grace, and the hope of glory? In short, do these traditions facilitate or hinder the sanctifying work of the Holy Spirit?

The third question takes up what the 1963 Montreal report of the Faith and Order Commission said about the call to find the Tradition (upper case and to be identified not simply with the whole Christian heritage but with Christ himself in person) in the particular traditions.[40] What traditions bring us closer to Christ in living as his disciples and in experiencing him as the primary minister of the sacraments and the High Priest of the Eucharistic assembly?

Fourthly and finally, our discernment should not only prove biblical (first question), pneumatological (second question), and Christological (third question) but also 'liturgical' (in the original sense of the term). In the New Testament and works of early Christian writers, *leitourgia* referred both to the community worship and to the obligation to meet the material needs of others. The double usage conveys the essential bond between worship and service of the suffering. Jesus expected his followers to help the hungry, the thirsty, strangers, the naked, the sick, and prisoners (Matt. 25: 31–46). His parable of the Good Samaritan powerfully illustrated what he wanted from all: the willingness to help any human being in distress (Luke 10: 30–7). The words of Jesus from Matthew 25 and Luke 10, along with the parable of the rich man and the poor Lazarus (Luke 16: 19–31), should touch the conscience of Christians involved in discerning traditions they have inherited from the past. Do these traditions support and embody Christ's call to minister to the destitute? Do they encourage us to recognize the crucified Jesus in those who suffer terrible need?

He identified himself with those who suffer from great affliction; they reveal the face of the crucified Christ. These suffering servants of today have much to say to us. A discernment that seeks to serve the poor must also be ready to hear the voice of the poor. A truly

[40] *Montreal 63*; see also 54, 57.

Christian discernment takes place at the foot of the cross. A discernment that ignores the cross cannot claim to be genuinely Christian.

These then are four questions that should guide Christians in discerning particular traditions in their search for *the* Tradition, not merely the apostolic Tradition but also Christ himself. What is he calling us to change, reform, or strengthen in all that we have received from the past? Any answers to this question are always the start of new questions. The question of discernment can never be answered adequately and once for all.

7

Achievements and Conclusions

This book has set itself to create a platform from which the cause of good tradition can be pleaded—always in relationship with the divine self-revelation in Jesus Christ and with the inspired Scriptures. The previous six chapters aimed at pulling their weight in establishing that platform.

(1) Firstly, for many years theological studies of the function and significance of Christian tradition have been extremely rare. The very few works that have appeared have examined, at best, only some limited aspects of tradition. In the 1960s a Montreal meeting of the Faith and Order Commission and then the Second Vatican Council illustrated a substantial consensus that had emerged between many Christian churches over the meaning and role of tradition. Chapter 1 above identified seven themes that created this consensus. One might have expected theologians to have followed up the work of Yves Congar, Gerhard Ebeling, Josef Rupert Geiselmann, Wolfhart Pannenberg, Joseph Ratzinger, and others who helped to effect and articulate the consensus. But theologians have, by and large, simply avoided reflection on tradition. The widely used *New Dictionary of Theology* symbolizes this common neglect.[1] It includes no entry on 'tradition', and does not even list 'tradition' in the index.

(2) Chapter 2, while attending also to Peter Berger and Anthony Giddens, retrieved four major proposals from Edward Shils about tradition. (a) We need to take a global or total view of tradition. It embodies everything societies and individuals inherit from the past.

[1] M. Davie et al. (eds), 2nd edn (Downer's Grove, IL: Inter-Varsity Press, 2016).

(b) Tradition identifies groups of people—not only initially but right through their lives. (c) We need to recognize the rich variety of agents who maintain and hand on traditions. (d) Sociologists can illuminate the processes involved when societies grapple with the authority and permanence of traditions. The community drops, reforms, maintains, and regenerates traditions in a constant process of discerning and reacting to what it has inherited. Present experience persistently interacts with patrimony inherited from the past.

Writing a generation later than Shils, Giddens highlights a huge force in the modern world that affects cultures and traditions (including Christian traditions): globalization in its various forms. Giddens emphasizes also the sweeping changes in traditional life-styles that have extended previous boundaries controlling the choices and behaviour of human beings. These new possibilities for self-actualization have accentuated the uncertainties of our 'runaway world'.

Christian theologians who dedicate their attention to tradition cannot afford to neglect the major insights and conclusions that sociologists offer. Experts in sociology have also encouraged me to offer unashamedly many specific examples. In the area of tradition, perhaps even more than in other theological sectors, mere abstractions cannot be allowed to replace vividly concrete images and narratives. Hence I have persistently introduced such specifics as the RCIA, the use of candles, sacred music and art (including icons), church buildings, the *camino* to Santiago de Compostela, and many further examples of healthy traditions.

(3) Chapter 3 was prompted by the conviction that understanding Christian tradition as either process or object will not be possible unless we grasp the basic characteristics of revelation as, primarily, involving a personal self-disclosure of the tripersonal God and as, secondarily, embodying this experience in traditions that are handed on. Thus revelation gave rise to the Scriptures, the celebration of baptism and the Eucharist, and innumerable other central or more peripheral elements in the history of Christian tradition. But, in the first instance, revelation meant the divine self-manifestation in Christ and through the Holy Spirit. Events of revelation, culminating in the resurrection of the crucified Jesus and the coming of the Holy Spirit, created the individual traditions that make up the whole 'treasure of revelation'.

Furthermore, to grasp the past, present, and future function of tradition, we need to take into account the biblical witness to revelation in a triple time-key—then, now, and to come. Tradition witnesses to a revelation that was the full and unsurpassable disclosure of the Son of God. But he is also the *Traditum* or *Christus praesens* at the heart of present revelation. His second coming will bring the definitive, self-manifestation of God that will be the end of human history and all the processes of tradition.

Chapter 3 went on to distinguish seven major characteristics of Christian tradition as process or *actus tradendi*. It is pre-given, with tradition always being part of us. We collectively inherit and are bound to tradition. It is richly polymorphous, displaying the huge diversity that is already there in divine self-revelation. It has a sacramental structure, blending things said and things done in order to mediate revelation and salvation. It regularly stands in tension with the present reality that we experience in our 'runaway world' (Anthony Giddens). It is constantly open to revision and reform. Finally, tradition forms a process that will end only with the close of human history.

As 'object' or *traditum*, tradition encompasses indefinitely many particular 'objects' that are transmitted. Chapter 3, like other chapters in this book, put on display something of this rich variety of traditions (plural and in lower case). Yet we should learn from the 1963 report of the Faith and Order Commission to highlight the essential *Traditum* (singular and upper case), Christ himself present through the Holy Spirit in the life of the Church. Understood as *Christus praesens*, Tradition is 'not an object which we possess but a reality by which we are possessed'. Christ is 'the living Tradition', living 'yesterday, today, and forever' (Heb. 13: 8) and supplying his followers with their essential self-definition.

The chapter ended by distinguishing tradition from the somewhat similar reality of *culture*. We face a certain equivalence: culture, for instance, also supplies something of the self-identity of a society or group. But tradition suggests much more interest in *historical origins* and the historical transmission of foundational experiences. One can happily describe tradition as the collective memory of that past. Tradition more than culture also prompts more attention to ways of *doing things* that are handed on from one generation to the next. Culture and tradition overlap, but they are not synonymous.

(4) Chapter 4 pursued the theme of *Christus praesens*, setting out twelve traditions (or groups of traditions) that embody or at least allude to the *Traditum*, who is *Christus praesens*. That roll call of traditions concludes with the Book of the Gospels, used in liturgical and extra-liturgical traditions to symbolize the presiding presence of the risen Jesus.

After indicating the wealth of official (e.g. the bishops) and 'unofficial' (e.g. artists and composers of sacred music) bearers and transmitters of Christian tradition, the chapter drew attention to the thirty-six doctors of the Church and to innumerable saintly men and women (whether canonized or not) whose powerful witness to faith in Christ made them outstanding in handing on the 'treasure' of tradition.

The chapter closed by reflecting on the Holy Spirit, the primary bearer of the Church's tradition, who transmits the faith by actualizing the union of the baptized with Christ and carrying forward their *sensus fidei* or *sensus fidelium*. It is through the Spirit that the *sensus fidelium* remains operative in the members of the Church.

(5) Chapter 5 brought us to the classical issue of the mutual dependence of Scripture and tradition, or what can be called the effective history (*Wirkungsgeschichte*) of the Bible. The living tradition interpreted and actualized the Scriptures but was also interpreted and challenged by them.

To illustrate this process, the chapter took up three examples: (a) the historical creeds which borrowed from the Scriptures to express the central biblical message of the Trinity; (b) the contrast between Adam and Christ as corporate representatives which began with Paul and enjoyed a rich development in liturgy, doctrine, art, and beyond; (c) the mutual impact of Scripture and tradition which attended the Reformation controversy over justification and which reached a substantive closure with the 1999 Joint Declaration on the Doctrine of Justification.

Chapter 5 concluded by examining two cases from the Second Vatican Council that illustrate the power of the Sacred Scriptures to correct long-standing, false traditions. First, the Declaration on Religious Freedom officially abandoned the traditional teaching that 'error has no rights', and, above all in the light of the respect for religious freedom shown by Jesus and his apostles, endorsed the freedom of conscience that belongs inalienably to every human being. Second, Vatican II became the first general council of Catholic Christianity to speak well of Jews. Paul's doctrine about God's irrevocable election of Israel helped to challenge and change centuries of teaching and practice tainted by anti-Semitism. Here as elsewhere, far more than old slogans, historical examples explain and enrich the way we see the interplay between Scripture and tradition.

(6) Edward Shils distinguished traditions that 'work' from those that experience shows 'do not work'. Chapter 6 (on 'Discerning Particular Traditions') opened by describing four traditions that have shown themselves to 'work': teaching about 'the seven deadly sins'; pilgrimages; the use of icons in worship and beyond; and the service of Nine Lessons and Carols. The chapter then expounded the case of a tradition that has not worked: the refusal of the sacraments to divorced Catholics who have been civilly remarried and remain sexually active. The 2016 exhortation from Pope Francis, *Amoris Laetitia*, set aside this blanket refusal and made it a matter of careful and prayerful discernment.

Shared pastoral experience and discernment actualize the community testing inculcated by 1 Thessalonians 5: 19–22 and 1 John 1: 4–6. Such discernment belongs to communities of worshipping Christians and should not be confined to individuals or small groups.

Along with contemporary experience, biblical teaching and post-New Testament developments should also guide any faithful discernment. The Second Vatican Council, when renewing, modifying, or abandoning traditions, was persistently guided by a sense of the apostolic witness: for instance, in introducing, or rather retrieving the tradition of collegiality that prevailed among the first leaders of the Church.

Furthermore, when engaged in testing and evaluating traditions they have inherited, Roman Catholics should also learn from their fellow Christians, other religious faiths, and the secular world. When Pope Francis recommended learning from fellow Christians (*Evangelii Gaudium*, 244, 246), he might have recalled the Second Vatican Council at which Anglican, Orthodox, and Protestant guests contributed really, albeit indirectly and discreetly, to the making of some of the sixteen documents. In several documents, Vatican II proposed taking on, even for purposes of worship (e.g. *SC* 37, 40, 119), some traditions and wisdom from the followers of other religions. Through interreligious dialogue, 'precious religious elements' and 'impulses of the Holy Spirit' (*GS* 92) can be received. Christians bent on renewing and reforming their traditions should also be open to truth coming from non-believers. Such 'outsiders' encouraged Vatican II into dropping opposition to religious freedom and producing *Dignitatis Humanae*. Pope Francis's encyclical on ecology and climate, *Laudato Si'*, displayed a readiness to be guided also by the findings of 'outside' groups such as the Food and Agriculture Organization.

Pope Francis's *Amoris Laetitia* exemplified another essential principle for discernment: a willingness to retrieve such forgotten traditions as the Eucharist being a 'medicine' for the weak and not a reward for the virtuous.

Finally, four questions bring together much that should guide the task of discerning existing traditions. What do the Scriptures suggest about maintaining or reforming specific traditions? Do these traditions help the faithful to be led effectively by the Holy Spirit? Do they bring them closer to Christ in their life and worship? What traditions or changes in traditions will prompt them into serving more generously the needy and suffering?

This chapter aimed at summarizing the results to be gleaned from the six chapters that form the heart of this book. Let me end by proposing its five major achievements.

- The 1963 Montreal conference of the Faith and Order Commission and the teaching of Vatican II represent an ecumenical convergence on the nature and function of Christian tradition.

- The social sciences—and, specifically, sociology—offer considerable help to those theologians who wish to explore and express tradition.

- The Christian tradition assumes innumerable forms, and any theology of tradition should attend to the richness of these traditions.

- The Scriptures play a major role for those who wish to discern the health or otherwise of existing tradition. But this discernment should also open itself to further criteria: for instance, those drawn from other Christian bodies, from other religions, and from the best insights of a non-believing, secular world.

• The heart of Christian tradition is *Christus praesens*, the *Traditum* ever actualized by the work of the Holy Spirit. Without using the language of tradition, Sandra Schneiders has written of the *Christus praesens* brought to us through traditional proclamation and the Eucharist: 'This experience of the glorified Jesus will be actualized every time the proclamation resounds, "It is the Lord", and the disciples, wearied from ministerial labours, sit down to table with him.'[2] More than a century ago, Albert Schweitzer also used John 21 to express hauntingly the personal reality at the heart of tradition:

> He comes to us as One unknown, without a name, as of old, by the lakeside, He came to those men who knew him not. He speaks to us the same word: 'Follow thou me!' and sets us to the tasks which He has to fulfil for our time. He commands. And to those who obey him, whether they be wise or simple, He will reveal himself in the toils, the conflicts, the sufferings which they shall pass through in His fellowship, and, as an ineffable mystery, they shall learn in their experience Who He is.[3]

---

[2] S. Schneiders, 'John 21: 2–14', *Interpretation* 43 (1989), 75.

[3] A. Schweitzer, *The Quest of the Historical Jesus: A Critical Study of Its Progress from Reimarus to Wrede*, 3rd edn (London: A. & C. Black, 1954; orig. German 1906), 401.

Appendix: Memory Studies and Tradition

The Second Vatican Council (1962–5) signalled a renewal in official Catholic teaching on the nature and function of tradition, a renewal not only expressed by *Dei Verbum*, the Dogmatic Constitution on Divine Revelation but also embodied in fifteen other documents produced by the Council, listed here in the order of their promulgation: *Sacrosanctum Concilium*, the Constitution on the Sacred Liturgy; *Inter Mirifica*, the Decree on the Means of Social Communication; *Lumen Gentium*, the Dogmatic Constitution on the Church; *Orientalium Ecclesiarum*, the Decree on the Eastern Catholic Churches; *Unitatis Redintegratio*, the Decree on Ecumenism; *Christus Dominus*, the Decree on the Pastoral Office of Bishops; *Perfectae Caritatis*, the Decree on the Renewal of Religious Life; *Optatam Totius*, the Decree on the Formation of Priests; *Gravissimum Educationis*, the Declaration on Christian Education; *Nostra Aetate*, the Declaration on the Relation of the Church to Non-Christian Religions; *Dei Verbum*, the Dogmatic Constitution on Divine Revelation; *Apostolicam Actuositatem*, the Decree on the Apostolate of Lay People; *Dignitatis Humanae*, the Decree on Religious Liberty; *Ad Gentes*, the Decree on the Church's Missionary Activity; *Presbyterorum Ordinis*, the Decree on the Ministry and Life of Priests; and *Gaudium et Spes*, the Pastoral Constitution on the Church in the Modern World. The promulgation of *Dei Verbum*, as René Latourelle observed, was 'the first time that any document of the extraordinary magisterium had proposed such an elaborate text on the nature, object and importance of tradition'.[1] But a study of Vatican II's integral teaching on tradition must *also* take into account what can be gleaned from other conciliar documents.[2]

While most of the Council's teaching on tradition remained focused on questions of specifically Christian tradition, at times the documents looked into the wider area of human tradition and traditions. Thus *Sacrosanctum Concilium* addressed the traditions of different peoples (*SC* 37–40), with particular respect to their traditions surrounding marriage (*SC* 77) and funerals (*SC* 81). *Ad Gentes* likewise attended to local traditions and cultures (*AG* 22). Much of what *Gaudium et Spes* said about culture implicitly dealt with human

---

[1] René Latourelle, *The Theology of Revelation: Including a Commentary on the Constitution Dei Verbum of Vatican II* (Cork: Mercier, 1968), 476.

[2] See David Braithwaite, 'Vatican II on Tradition', *Heythrop Journal* 53 (2012), 915–28.

tradition (*GS* 53–62). In both specifically Christian and wider human culture, any tradition, we should add, must be *remembered* tradition if it is going to be effective.

Although the key Vatican II chapter on tradition does not as such introduce the theme of memory (*DV* 7–10), other texts of the Council recall much that the Church remembers. At the heart of her life, the Constitution on the Sacred Liturgy recognizes the Eucharist, the great 'memorial' of the death and resurrection of Jesus Christ (*SC* 47). Each Sunday the Church celebrates collectively the 'memory' of the Lord's resurrection; on Good Friday and Easter Sunday, she recalls with the 'greatest solemnity' his death and rising from the dead (*SC* 102; see also 106). Whether within the liturgy itself or beyond it in daily life, all the baptized should 'remember the cross and resurrection of the Lord' (*Apostolicam Actuositatem* no. 4). Entering the Church means dying, being buried, and rising with Christ, so as to 'celebrate with the whole people of God the memorial of the death and resurrection of the Lord' (*AG* 14). Thus the Eucharist collectively keeps alive the central memory that identifies and defines Christian existence: the passion, death, and resurrection of Jesus. In the words of the 1994 *Catechism of the Catholic Church*, 'primarily in the Eucharist, and by analogy in the other sacraments, the liturgy is *the memorial* of the mystery of salvation'.[3]

Vatican II remembers other great themes lodged in the memory of the Church: for instance, the deep spiritual link between 'the people of the New Testament and the stock of Abraham'. It is because she 'remembers her common heritage with the Jews' that the Church deplores all anti-Semitism (*NA* 4). The Council also invokes the shared memory of different words from the Lord to motivate various attitudes and actions: mutual love within the Christian community (*GS* 93), a concern for the mission to the world (*LG* 16), and appropriate activity on the part of bishops (*LG* 27), priests (*Presbyterorum Ordinis*, 5), and lay persons (*Apostolicam Actuositatem*, 4).

Finally, Vatican II introduced the language of collective memory when it confirmed the importance of the 'memorial days' of the martyrs and other saints (*SC* 104), and evoked the union with the heavenly church realized in the liturgy. There 'we remember the glorious Mary ever Virgin, blessed Joseph, the blessed apostles, martyrs, and all the saints' (*LG* 50).

In short, the Second Vatican Council (a) employed the language of 'memory', 'remembering', and 'memorials' and (b) treated 'tradition' and particular 'traditions'. But it never explicitly brought together (a) and (b).

---

[3] *The Catechism of the Catholic Church* (Vatican City: Libreria Editrice Vaticana, 1994), no.1099; emphasis added.

Tradition as Collective Memory

As the work of Vatican II drew to a close, some theologians did, however, invoke tradition and, specifically, the human reality of tradition when speaking (briefly) of tradition as collective memory. In a work that appeared during the Council, Yves Congar wrote, 'Tradition is memory and memory enriches experience.'[4] He went on to talk of the Church's memory: 'The Church not only possesses self-awareness; she keeps and actualizes the living memory of what she has received.'[5] 'The living memory' was obviously intended to echo 'living tradition', an expression cherished by nineteenth-century theologians of Tübingen[6] and their successors and eventually inserted into *Dei Verbum* (art. 12). George Tavard agreed with Congar: 'One could analyse tradition from the standpoint of memory and define it as the Church's memory.'[7]

In a 1974 essay, 'Anthropological Foundation of the Concept of Tradition', Joseph Ratzinger examined the human phenomenon of tradition, arguing that 'intellect is basically memory', and that 'memory generates tradition'.[8] In another essay, originally published in 1975, Ratzinger stated that 'the decisive question for today is whether that memory [and the tradition it has generated] can continue to exist through which the Church becomes church and without which she sinks into nothingness'.[9]

In the next decade Jean-Marie-Roger Tillard dedicated a section of his ecclesiology to 'the memory of the church'[10] and called tradition 'a function of remembrance'. Far from envisaging any possibility of the Church 'sinking into nothingness', he maintained that 'as the memory of the Church, tradition

---

[4] Yves Congar, *Tradition and the Life of the Church*, trans. A. N. Woodrow (London: Burns & Oates, 1964; orig. French 1963), 8.

[5] Ibid. 77.

[6] On Johann Sebastian Drey's idea of 'living tradition', see John E. Thiel, *Senses of Tradition: Continuity and Development of Catholic Faith* (New York: Oxford University Press, 2000), 59–63; on Johann Adam Möhler's organic model of tradition, see ibid. 63–7.

[7] George H. Tavard, 'Tradition in Theology: A Problematic Approach', in Joseph F. Kelly (ed.), *Perspectives on Scripture and Tradition* (Notre Dame, IN: Fides, 1976), 84–104, at 92.

[8] Joseph Ratzinger, 'Anthropological Foundation of the Concept of Tradition', in *Principles of Catholic Theology: Building Stones for a Fundamental Theology*, trans. Frances McCarthy (San Francisco: Ignatius Press, 1987), 85–101, at 86–7.

[9] Joseph Ratzinger, 'What Constitutes Christian Faith Today?', in ibid. 15–27, at 24.

[10] J.-M.-R. Tillard, *Church of Churches: The Ecclesiology of Communion*, trans. R. C. De Peaux (Collegeville, MN: Liturgical Press, 1987), 140–4.

represents the permanence of a Word which is always alive, always enriched, and yet radically always the same, where the Church never ceases to nourish its faith'.[11]

A biblical theme about the Holy Spirit 'reminding' the disciples of 'all that I [Jesus] have said to you' (John 14: 26) obviously encouraged a theology that expounded tradition as memory. The *Catechism of the Catholic Church* could firmly state not only that 'the Holy Spirit awakens the memory of the Church' and 'in the liturgy of the word recalls to the assembly all that Christ has done for us' (art. 1103), but also that 'the Holy Spirit *is* the Church's living memory' (art. 1099; emphasis added). In at least three documents, John Paul II introduced the theme of tradition as collective memory but without explicitly identifying the Spirit as the Church's living memory: *Catechesi Tradendae* of 1979 (art. 22), *Orientale Lumen* of 1995 (art. 8), and *Ecclesia in Europa* of 2003 (art. 7–8).[12]

Some post-Vatican II studies of tradition, to be sure, do not reflect on tradition as the collective memory of the Church.[13] But those who followed Congar in doing so (Ratzinger, Tavard, and Tillard) seemed, like him, to remain unaware of a huge development of studies about memory (and forgetting) in anthropology, history, neuroscience, philosophy, psychology, and sociology.[14] Some or even much of this work consciously looks back to the French sociologist Maurice Halbwachs, who began publishing on collective memory in 1925.[15] Scriptural scholars have happily drawn on modern

---

[11] Ibid. 141, 142.

[12] The Vatican website publishes all three documents. They are also available in various printed forms: e.g. in *Acta Apostolicae Sedis*.

[13] For instance, Thiel's *Senses of Tradition* (2000) contains nothing about tradition as the memory of the Church; neither does Dietrich Wiederkehr (ed.), *Wie geschieht Tradition? Überlieferung im Lebensprozess der Kirche* (Freiburg: Herder, 1991); nor does Thomas Langan, *The Catholic Tradition* (Columbia: University of Missouri Press, 1998).

[14] A welcome exception was Joseph G. Mueller, 'Forgetting as a Principle of Continuity in Tradition', *Theological Studies* 70 (2009), 751–81.

[15] See e.g. Maurice Halbwachs, *On Collective Memory*, trans. Lewis A. Coser (Chicago: University of Chicago Press, 1992). A (very) select list of modern studies on collective memory could include such works as Edward S. Casey, *Remembering: A Phenomenological Study* (Bloomington: Indiana University Press, 1987); Paul Connerton, *How Societies Remember* (New York: Cambridge University Press, 1989); Paul Connerton, *How Modernity Forgets* (New York: Cambridge University Press, 2009); James Fentress and Chris Wickham, *Social Memory* (Oxford: Blackwell, 1992); Barbara A. Misztal, *Theories of Social Remembering* (Philadelphia: Open University Press, 2003); Pierre Nora (ed.), *Realms of Memory*, 3 vols, trans. Arthur Goldhammer

memory studies.[16] But theologians have, almost universally, failed to draw on those studies and take advantage of insights that could illuminate and enrich work on tradition.

Studies of Collective Memory: Twelve Applications to the Theology of Tradition

In the fairly recent past, many sociologists and others tended to take a negative view of collective memory. As Barry Schwartz puts it, 'believing all realities to be socially constructed, a generation of scholars depreciated collective memory'. But Schwartz and other more recent writers have rejected the blanket view that collective memory *merely* reconstructs the past, adapts historical facts to the beliefs and spiritual needs of the present, or even creates such 'facts'. Rather he argues that as 'an intrinsic part of culture, collective memory works in tandem with science, politics, religion, art, and common sense to interpret experience'.[17] Beyond question, memory, collective or otherwise, is invariably and inevitably selective, simplified, and structured; it can be consciously manipulated, and frequently lapses into forgetfulness. Nevertheless, in various ways it also operates under the constraints of history. Memory reflects, as well as shapes, social reality. Its claims to represent the past faithfully may not be dismissed out of hand. There is some legitimacy in the historical knowledge carried by collective memory.[18]

Recent memory studies coming from such scholars as Paul Connerton, James Fentress, Paul Ricoeur, Barry Schwartz, and Chris Wickham have encouraged us to apply to Christian tradition their conclusions about the nature and role of collective (or social) memory. Collective memory can perform a

---

(New York: Columbia University Press, 1996–8); Paul Ricoeur, *Memory, History, Forgetting*, trans. Kathleen Blamey and David Pellauer (Chicago: University of Chicago Press, 2004); Michael Schudson, *Watergate in American Memory: How We Remember, Forget, and Reconstruct the Past* (New York: Basic Books, 1992); Barry Schwartz, *Abraham Lincoln and the Forge of National Memory* (Chicago: University of Chicago Press, 2000).

[16] See e.g. James D. G. Dunn, *Jesus Remembered* (Grand Rapids, MI: Eerdmans, 2003); Rafael Rodriguez, *Structuring Early Christian Memory: Jesus in Tradition, Performance, and Text* (London: T. & T. Clark, 2010); and Loren T. Stuckenbruck, Stephen C. Barton, and Benjamin G. Wold (eds), *Memory in the Bible and Antiquity* (Tübingen: Mohr Siebeck, 2007).

[17] Schwarz, *Abraham Lincoln*, x, xi.

[18] As the title hints, much of Ricoeur's *Memory, History, Forgetting* is devoted to the place of history in memory, collective or personal.

properly systematic role in uniting and clarifying various aspects of a Christian theology of tradition. Let us present twelve ways in which memory studies might have this happy result. The first concerns the very legitimacy of the term 'collective memory'.

(1) While it may be natural to think primarily of memory as 'an individual faculty', Connerton remarks that many thinkers 'concur in believing that there is some such thing as a collective or social memory'.[19] Anthropologist Clifford Geertz describes culture in terms that also fit collective memory—as a pattern of 'inherited conceptions expressed in symbolic forms by means of which people communicate, perpetuate, and develop their knowledge about and attitudes toward life'.[20] Without going as far as Halbwachs, who held that 'all memory is structured by group identities' and that hence 'memories are essentially group memories', Fentress and Wickham observed that 'much memory is attached to membership of social groups of one kind or another'.[21] They agreed that 'in and of itself, memory is simply subjective', or the property of individual human beings. Nevertheless, 'memory is structured by language, by teaching and observing, by collectively held ideas, and by experiences shared with others'.[22] In particular, shared memories justify speaking of social or collective memory.

Far from being isolated individuals, people acquire their memories through living in society; when they recall and 'place' their memories, they also do this in society. Jeffrey K. Olick, a sociologist who drew on and modified the thought of Halbwachs, has continued to stress the intersubjective nature of memory: 'There is no individual memory without social experience, nor is there any collective memory without individuals participating in communal life.'[23] Individuals and society are not separate things—neither vis-à-vis memory nor in other ways.

Theologians would not then prove to be odd persons out if they were to characterize Christian tradition as collective memory. Such a view enjoys an antecedent plausibility from memory studies in other disciplines. Those studies, admittedly, often do not introduce the term 'tradition'. Connerton, Fentress and Wickham, and Schwartz, for instance, do not list any reference to 'tradition' in their indexes. Ricoeur's 642-page book contains 48 references

[19] Connerton, *How Societies Remember*, 36–40.

[20] Clifford Geertz, 'Religion as a Cultural System', *The Interpretation of Cultures* (New York: Basic Books, 1973), 87–125, at 89.

[21] Fentress and Wickham, *Social Memory*, ix.   [22] Ibid. 7.

[23] J. K. Olick, 'Collective Memory: The Two Cultures', *Sociological Theory* 17 (1999), 333–48, at 346.

to collective memory but only one to tradition.[24] Nevertheless, collectively remembering the past obviously involves collectively receiving, narrating, (often) revising, and reliving a tradition or some traditions. Receiving, narrating, revising, and reliving a tradition are inconceivable without remembering the past.

(2) What we quoted above from Geertz and Halbwachs illustrates how anthropologists, sociologists, and other scholars regularly describe collective memory in *all-encompassing* terms. It embraces the intellectual, emotional, moral, and religious frameworks of human life. One would expect the tradition created and transmitted by the memory of a religious group to have a similar *total* character. Albeit without referencing any modern memory studies, Vatican II not surprisingly presented tradition as all-encompassing: 'in her doctrine, life, and worship, the Church perpetuates and transmits to every generation all that she herself is, all that she herself believes' (*DV* 8).

(3) Fentress, Wickham, and others who have contributed to memory studies understand memory to express 'an active search for meaning'. In particular, in its quest for meaning through memory a group finds meaning in the past and relives 'its past in the present'. 'Social memories' exist because they 'relate closely' to the 'collective self-images'.[25] This group *search for meaning*, which involves reliving the past in the present, establishes and clarifies *identity*. Thus 'memory has an immense social role. It tells us who we are.'[26] The collectively remembered past clarifies for human beings their personal and group identity, which is always an identity-in-relationship. Collective memory plays its role in sustaining *group identity*, whether we deal with small, face-to-face societies or with a world religion whose members personally know only a limited number of others.

Remembering Jesus provides the whole Christian community with the essential meaning for their lives, their basic identity, and a *raison d'être* or main reason for their existence. In that radical sense, the Church is a 'community of memory'.[27] Here some words from Ratzinger (see above), 'memory generates tradition', find their supreme exemplification. The memory of Jesus has generated the Christian tradition *tout court.*

Their collective experience of the memory of Jesus continues to tell Christians who they are and to define their identity-in-relationship to him and to

---

[24] Ricoeur, *Memory, History, Forgetting*, 636, 641.

[25] Fentress and Wickham, *Social Memory*, 73, 97. As Schwartz remarks, 'collective memory is part of culture's meaning-making apparatus' (*Abraham Lincoln*, 17).

[26] Fentress and Wickham, *Social Memory*, 201.

[27] Robert N. Bellah et al., *Habits of the Heart* (New York: Harper & Row, 1985), 227, 229.

the founding fathers and mothers of the Church, as well as to those figures in the Christian past who represent the highest values for them. Thus a collective memory at the heart of tradition defines and explains the identity of Christians. Sharing and handing down primarily (a) the distant memory of Jesus and the founding generations of the Church and secondarily (b) the more recent memory of heroic figures (for instance, Francis and Clare of Assisi) preserve and nourish the religious identity of Christians. It is above all that distant memory (a) which identifies and maintains their collective memory and the stability of the 'faith that comes to us from the apostles' (First Eucharistic Prayer). Eucharistic prayers also regularly recall martyrs and saints from a more recent memory (b). Both the distant and the more recent memory keep in existence and shape the collective memory that has created the basic Christian tradition and identity.

Congar, who led the way in associating memory and tradition, has remarked, 'Tradition is like the consciousness of a group or *the principle of identity* which links one generation to another; it enables them to remain . . . the same people as they go forward through history.' In short, tradition is 'a principle that ensures . . . continuity and identity'.[28] Congar rightly links memory/tradition with identity and continuity; modern memory studies can develop and enrich his insights. He also brings us to a third theme found in those studies: the role of memory (and tradition) in ensuring not only group identity but also a closely connected characteristic: continuity.

(4) Collective memory is crucial in sustaining the link between past, present, and future required by authentic *continuity*. Thus an anthropologist (Fentress) and a historian (Wickham) begin by linking past and present: 'we experience the present as connected to the past. Our experience of the present is thus embedded in past experience.'[29] They press on to highlight the role of collective memory in upholding the continuity between past, present, and future: social memory expresses 'collective experience; social memory identifies a group, giving it a sense of its past and defining its aspirations for the future'.[30] Thus memory 'is not merely retrospective; it is prospective as well'.[31]

---

[28] Congar, *Tradition and the Life of the Church*, 8, emphasis added and translation corrected. When reflecting (very briefly) on collective identity, Congar does not consider a collective *identity crisis*, which might be faced and overcome by reappropriating illuminating and life-giving memories from the past and the traditions they created.

[29] Fentress and Wickham, *Social Memory*, 24. 　　　[30] Ibid. 25.

[31] Ibid. 51.

Here an antiphon composed by Thomas Aquinas for the feast of Corpus Christi readily comes to mind. It embodies the triple time-sign of collective memory, in this case of Eucharistic remembrance: 'O sacred banquet in which Christ is received: his suffering is remembered [past], [our] mind is filled with grace [present], and we receive a pledge of glory that is to be ours [future] [*O sacrum convivium, in quo Christus sumitur, recolitur memoria passionis eius, mens impletur gratia, et futurae gloriae nobis pignus datur*].'

In an essay first published in 1974, Ratzinger reflected briefly on the same link between past, present, and future, even if he spoke of unity rather than continuity: 'Memory works to give meaning by establishing unity, by communicating the past to the present, and by providing a mode of access to the future.'[32] Connerton specifies a central Christian activity that secures such essential continuity by conveying and sustaining collective memory (and tradition): the ritual performances that believers constantly experience.[33] Commemorative ceremonies, like baptism and the Eucharist, embody and maintain essential continuity in the Christian tradition. By ritually re-enacting such events as the baptism of Jesus and his Last Supper and, it is to be hoped, nourishing a life-style required by the grace and meaning of those basic sacraments, Christian memory serves the continuity of tradition. If one asks where and how collective memory and the tradition it has generated continue to operate in the Church, her festivities and sacramental life must bulk large in any answer.

(5) In a discussion that enriches a theological treatment of tradition, Connerton considers 'bodily practices' to be essential in transmitting the collective memory of any group.[34] In one way or another, all social memory is passed on through bodily practices, not least through language. In the case of Christian tradition, passing on social memory constitutes one of the main purposes of language: in preaching, catechesis, the performance of liturgical texts, the singing of hymns, religious publishing, and so forth. Here it is important to recall this, even though the linguistic transmission of collective memory will come up under (7) below.

Christian collective memory is expressed and transmitted not only through such traditional bodily practices as making the sign of the cross and various gestures embodied in all the sacraments but also through such feasts as Christmas, Holy Thursday, Good Friday, and the Easter Vigil, all of which are unimaginable without traditional bodily practices. They include building and visiting Christmas crèches, washing the feet of people, venerating the

[32] Ratzinger, 'Anthropological Foundation', 88.
[33] Connerton, *How Societies Remember*, 41–71.   [34] Ibid. 72–104.

cross, standing around an Easter fire, and entering a church holding lighted candles. Here it is at our peril that we ignore the bodily practice involved in processions and pilgrimages. Nowadays Christians of different denominations often participate in a Good Friday procession through the streets of their village, town, or city. In a more extended 'bodily practice', many go on pilgrimage to Bethlehem, Guadalupe, Jerusalem, Lourdes, Rome, Santiago de Compostela, Walsingham, and the island of Tinos, where Orthodox Christians celebrate in a special way the 'dormition' (or falling asleep in death) of the Blessed Virgin Mary. These and other traditional places of pilgrimage have been consecrated by the collective memories and 'bodily practices' of Christians. All such bodily practices help 'keep the past in mind'.[35] Connerton's thesis richly illuminates the transmission of the tradition that Christian memory has created and preserves.

Halbwachs, founder of modern collective memory studies, maintained that 'if a truth is to be settled in the memory of a group, it needs to be presented in the concrete form of an event, of a personality [*d'une figure personelle*], or of a locality'.[36] Pilgrimages brilliantly exemplify this view. Their goal is a locality, bound up with some central personality and an event in which that person was involved: for instance, Bethlehem (the birth of Jesus), the Sea of Galilee (the scene of much of his preaching), the holy sepulchre in Jerusalem (his death, burial, and resurrection), and Rome (the martyrdom of Peter, Paul, and others).[37] Many, if not all, pilgrimages involve all three elements that Halbwachs considered essential for the emergence of a group memory (which generates an enduring tradition): a locality, a personality, and some event.

(6) We have already picked out continuity as characteristic of collective memory and the tradition it creates (see (4) above). For it to survive and prosper, such continuity must be open to constant *revision* and *reform*. Schwarz remarks that 'memory affects the way people interpret what is happening to them'.[38] But what happens to them as individuals and groups constantly

---

[35] Ibid. 72. Connerton dedicates some pages to pilgrimage in his later book, *How Modernity Forgets*, 14–18.

[36] Halbwachs, *On Collective Memory*, 200.

[37] Vatican II documents used pilgrimage language: the noun *peregrinatio*, the verb *peregrinor*, and the adjective *peregrinus*. But it used that language metaphorically: of (a) the baptized being on 'pilgrimage toward eternal beatitude' (*LG* 12) or 'on pilgrimage toward the kingdom of the Father' (*GS* 1); and of (b) the Church as such being a 'pilgrim' church (*LG* 6, 48; *UR* 6). The Council's texts came closest to a literal sense when speaking of 'Israel according to the flesh' being 'on pilgrimage in the desert' (*LG* 9).

[38] Schwartz, *Abraham Lincoln*, 20.

changes. Such changing conditions must be matched by constant revisions in memories, if those memories (and the traditions they give rise to) are going to continue serving the spiritual and other needs of people. In his substantial study, Schwartz illustrates how the image of Abraham Lincoln, from his assassination through to the end of the twentieth century, underwent steady revision while remaining under the constraints of historical evidence. The Church's collective memories must be open to a similar revision, while preserving an appropriate stability, if they are to continue serving the spiritual needs of Catholics and other Christians.

Here a key question concerns the 'appropriate stability'. What is it and how do we recognize it? Vatican II moved this question to the centre of attention, since it set itself to revising the Church's collective memories and changing various practices in the light of that revision. Some interpret that revision and changed practice by appealing to a scheme of permanent principles and altered forms. We understand such revision as contributing to appropriate stability by regaining and renewing the apostolic identity of the Church.[39]

(7) Halbwachs understood language to be 'the most elementary and the most stable framework of collective memory'.[40] Where he wrote of 'social frameworks', Jan Assmann spoke of 'semantic frames'.[41] Translating memories into language through a desire to communicate, groups must conform to conventional semantic frameworks if they are to make memories intelligible, interpret their significance, and pass them on successfully. Memories give rise to language and texts.

To be sure, from the early centuries Christians also translated and expressed their collective memories in other ways—for instance, through visual images embodied in art and architecture. Paintings, sculptures, and church buildings incorporated such memories. But before that happened, Christians expressed their memories of Jesus and the founding events in the life of the Church through oral stories and written texts—above all, the four Gospels and the other books of the New Testament that were eventually to be enshrined in the canon of inspired Scriptures.

Here we should recognize how the founding memories of Christianity also took their shape from the textual corpus of the Old Testament. That

---

[39] See Gerald O'Collins, 'Does Vatican II Represent Continuity or Discontinuity?', *Theological Studies* 73 (2012), 768–94, at 791–4.

[40] Halbwachs, *On Collective Memory*, 45.

[41] Jan Assmann, 'Ancient Egyptian Antijudaism: A Case of Distorted Memory', in Daniel L. Schachter (ed.), *Memory Distortion: How Minds, Brains, and Societies Reconstruct the Past* (Cambridge, MA: Harvard University Press, 1995), 365–78, at 366.

pre-existing body of texts provided an elementary and stable framework for understanding and interpreting the memories of Jesus and the founding events of Christianity. What had taken place was understood to have happened 'according to the Scriptures'.

Thus modern memory studies prove their value in describing and explaining the genesis of the Christian Scriptures—not to mention the Hebrew Bible. Those texts emerged from the traditions generated by the personal and group memories of Jesus and the various founding events and figures of Christianity. Vatican II helpfully presented tradition and the Scriptures as coming from the same source (revelation), functioning together in the life of the Church, and moving towards the same final goal (*DV* 9). What has been proposed by Halbwachs and his successors underscores even more the radical union between (a) the stable framework of the Scriptures and (b) the collective memory or tradition from which they emerged.

(8) Modern memory studies have recalled what ought to be seen as an obvious truism: 'forgetting is normal'.[42] What holds good at the level of personal memory also applies to collective memory. Groups can and do forget, and that belongs to the way memory regularly operates. To his philosophical study of memory and history, Ricoeur adds a section on forgetting.[43] Joseph Mueller, a theologian who stands more or less alone in drawing on modern studies of memory to explicate tradition, rightly recognized the inevitable role of 'collective forgetting'.[44]

(9) Schwartz's study of the collective memories of Abraham Lincoln shows throughout how remembered images of the dead president have oriented people towards thinking and acting in appropriate ways. They have not only reverenced the memory of Lincoln but have also been drawn to emulate him by seeing and practising ideals he communicated. He has helped fashion a symbolic framework that enabled Americans to make sense of their world and commit themselves accordingly. In Schwartz's words, Lincoln 'became America's universal man, changing and remaining the same; standing beside the people and above the people; a reflection of them *and model for them*'.[45]

Memory presents past persons and events as (traditional) objects for *emulation* and *commitment*. Remembering the past makes it a programme for commitment in the present. Whether we think of such traditions as the daily

[42] Fentress and Wickham, *Social Memory*, 39.

[43] Ricoeur, *Memory, History, Forgetting*, 412–56. After publishing his work on *Social Memory* in 1989, Connerton subsequently added in 2009 a brilliant study, *How Modernity Forgets*; see n. 15 above.

[44] Mueller, 'Forgetting as a Principle of Continuity in Tradition'.

[45] Schwartz, *Abraham Lincoln*, 312, emphasis added.

celebration of the Eucharist or an annual pilgrimage to Padua for the feast of Saint Anthony on 13 June, collective memories help the faithful glimpse how they should think about themselves and commit themselves. In particular, so much of the past retrieved by the documents of Vatican II works to provide values and aspirations that should underpin fresh commitments in the present. To take one among innumerable examples, the opening chapter of *Ad Gentes* (art. 2–9) introduced quotations from or references to twenty-three Church fathers, some of them, such as Irenaeus and Augustine, more than once. This chapter retrieved from the Christian tradition remarkable texts that continue to inspire and guide the missionary activity of the whole Church.

(10) There is a further area in which studying social or collective memory could yield valuable insights about human and Christian tradition. In the history of general councils of the Church, Vatican II broke new ground by attending to and promoting the traditions of different peoples (*SC* 37–40; *AG* 22). Without using the term 'inculturation', the Council wanted the traditions of various ethnic, local, and regional communities to help shape the Catholic celebration of marriages (*SC* 77), funerals (*SC* 81), and so forth. Notoriously the colonial period of European expansion, often without discerning what was illuminating and life-giving and what was false and destructive, disparaged and condemned much that shaped local traditions, especially in the area of religious beliefs and practices. Vatican II invested with a justified dignity certain traditions and the memory of such traditions. The Council did not, of course, express matters in this way. But at least two of its documents, *Sacrosanctum Concilium* and *Ad Gentes*, took a positive attitude towards the possibility of a genuine 'preparation for the Gospel' (*AG* 3) being found in particular human traditions and the collective memory that had created and transmitted such traditions.[46] This was to recognize and heal what Ricoeur calls the wounds 'stored in the archives of the collective memory'.[47]

(11) Ricoeur reminds us that collective memory and the traditions which it inspires can prove pathological, even dangerously pathological. Ricoeur calls such memory 'haunted', a 'past that does not pass', 'collective traumatisms', or 'wounds to the collective memory'.[48] At times such pathological memories derive from 'acts of violence' that founded the history and traditions of some ethnic or national group.[49] Modern memory studies have much to offer about the pathology that can affect memory.

---

[46] See Gerald O'Collins, *The Second Vatican Council on Other Religions* (Oxford: Oxford University Press, 2013), 78–9, 113–16.

[47] Ricoeur, *Memory, History, Forgetting*, 79.

[48] Ibid. 54, 78.   [49] Ibid. 79.

In *Unitatis Redintegratio*, its Decree on Ecumenism, Vatican II acknowledged that 'every renewal of the Church essentially consists in an increased fidelity to her vocation'. In fact, 'the Church is called by Christ' to 'a constant reformation, which she invariably needs inasmuch as she is a human and earthly institution' (*UR* 6). The collective memory of the Church (along with traditions to which that memory gives rise) can suffer from pathological wounds (e.g. hostility to other Christians and followers of other religions). The discerning and constant reformation of particular traditions also invites a certain purification of collective memory and the healing of memory's wounds—a theme not developed by the Decree on Ecumenism.

The purification of harmful memories played a striking role in the pontificate of St John Paul II (pope 1978–2005). He repeatedly asked Jews, Orthodox Christians, Protestants, and other groups to forgive crimes committed against them by Catholics. On the First Sunday of Lent 2000 in St Peter's Basilica, he underlined the need to face the wounds of memory. The confession of sins at the Eucharist on that Sunday featured seven representatives of the Roman Curia asking pardon for such sins as intolerance, anti-Semitism, discrimination against women, and contempt for various cultures and religions. Such wounds in the group identity of Catholic Christians have left toxic memories. The constant reformation of the Church proposed by *Unitatis Redintegratio* involves recalling and seeking healing for wounds in the collective memory.

(12) Finally, Congar's writing of the collective 'self-awareness' of the Church raises a question about collective consciousness and its subject.[50] Talk of collective memory transposes personal memory to the group level and almost inevitably leads one to ask: Whose memory is it? Is there a transcendent self who exercises this collective consciousness and memory? The language of the *Catechism of the Catholic Church* ('the Holy Spirit is the church's living memory')[51] could encourage one to think of the Spirit as the transcendent subject of the Church's collective memory. The Spirit would then not only awaken this memory but also prove to be the subject exercising this memory.

Congar himself spoke of the Holy Spirit not only as 'the soul of the Church' who 'creates, from within, the unity of the community and its tradition',[52] but also as 'the transcendent subject of Tradition'.[53] Here Congar built on the chapter dedicated to tradition in *Dei Verbum* (art. 7–10) with its language about

---

[50] See Congar, *Tradition and the Life of the Church.*   [51] No. 1099.

[52] Yves Congar, *Tradition and Traditions: A Historical and Theological Essay*, trans. Michael Naseby and Thomas Rainborough (London: Burns & Oates 1966), 340.

[53] Ibid. 338.

the Holy Spirit 'leading believers to the full truth and making the Word of God dwell in them in all its richness' (*DV* 8). The repeated appeal in that chapter to the Spirit's help in faithfully transmitting the Gospel has encouraged commentators to understand the Spirit as the primary Agent of tradition or 'the invisible bearer of tradition'.[54]

To recognize the Holy Spirit as the primary Agent of tradition and the invisible Subject of the collective memory that constitutes tradition brings up the question: Is the Spirit then somehow responsible for the wounds in the collective memory that call for purification and healing (theme (11) above)?[55] One might reply that the holiness of the primary Agent of tradition and invisible Subject of the Church's collective memory is not jeopardized by the wounds left by the sins of the secondary agents of that tradition and the human community which constitutes the visible subject of a collective memory. After all, Paul wrote about the Holy Spirit 'dwelling in you [plural]' (1 Cor. 3: 16) and making the Christian community the temple of the Spirit, while using the same letter to call on the community to face up to various sins that had wounded them and needed healing.

In a similar way the image of the Church as the Body of Christ presents all the baptized forming an organic unity with the all-holy Lord from whom their life flows. Yet the members of the Church can wound that body through their sinful weakness.

Conclusion

This appendix has suggested twelve developments for a theology of tradition that could draw and adapt insights from modern memory studies: (1) the basic legitimacy of the language of 'collective memory'; (2) the all-encompassing nature of collective memory; (3) the role such memory plays in sustaining group identity; (4) its role in securing continuity; (5) the transmission of collective memory through 'bodily practices'; (6) the constant revision and reform of collective memory; (7) the texts such memory gives rise to; (8) the inevitable function of 'forgetting'; (9) the emulation and commitment supported by collective memories and the traditions they create; (10) facing harmful memories through now accepting the inculturation of the Gospel;

---

[54] Gerald O'Collins and Edward G. Farrugia, 'Tradition', *A Concise Dictionary of Theology*, 3rd edn (Mahwah, NJ: Paulist Press, 2013), 246–7, at 246.

[55] In *True and False Reform in the Church*, trans. Paul Philibert (Collegeville, MN: Liturgical Press, 2011; orig. French 1950), Yves Congar wrote about 'collective responsibility' for evil and, albeit without using explicitly the language of 'collective memory', recalled how evil has also affected the life and memory of the Church (349–64).

(11) confronting toxic memories that have left wounds in the collective identity of the Church; and (12) the transcendent subject of Christians' collective memory, the Holy Spirit.

When we introduce what memory studies contribute to a theology of tradition, each of the twelve 'contributions' we have identified points to what, in one sense or another, we already know. All these contributions can be unified through the single concept of collective memory. In that way memory studies work to provide a properly systematic view, since their concept of collective memory functions to unite and clarify twelve aspects of a theology of tradition.

In proposing this enrichment of the theology of tradition, we have not drawn from one contributor to modern memory studies but from a number of representative authors who have worked and written in a variety of disciplines. If what we have argued above stands up, these specialists can help us exploit the theme of collective memory and develop more fully the brief suggestions made years ago by Congar and others when naming tradition as collective memory.[56]

---

[56] This appendix, co-authored by Gerald O'Collins and David Braithwaite, originally appeared in *Theological Studies* 76 (2015), 29–42, and is reprinted with permission from Sage Publications.

Select Bibliography

Baumann, M. et al., 'Tradition', in H. D. Betz et al. (eds), *Religion in Geschichte und Gegenwart*, 4th edn, viii (Tübingen: Mohr Siebcck, 2005), 505–21.

Beck, U., A. Giddens, and S. Lash, *Reflexive Modernization: Politics, Tradition and Aesthetics in Modern Social Order* (Cambridge: Polity Press, 1994).

Berger, P. L., *The Heretical Imperative: Contemporary Possibilities of Religious Affirmation* (London: Collins, 1980).

Betti, U., *La trasmissione della divina rivelazione* (Rome: Antonianum Press, 1985).

Biemer, G., *Newman on Tradition* (London: Burns & Oates, 1967).

Boeglin, J. G., *La question de la tradition dans la théologie catholique contemporaine* (Paris: Cerf, 1998).

Boyer, P., *Tradition as Truth and Communication: A Cognitive Description of Traditional Discourse* (Cambridge: Cambridge University Press, 1990).

Braithwaite, D., 'Vatican II on Tradition', *Heythrop Journal* 53 (2012), 915–28.

Brown, D., *Tradition and Imagination: Revelation and Change* (Oxford: Oxford University Press, 1999).

Congar, Y., *Tradition and the Life of the Church*, trans. A. N. Woodrow (London: Burns & Oates, 1964).

Congar, Y., *Tradition and Traditions: An Historical and Theological Essay*, trans. M. Naseby and T. Rainborough (London: Burns & Oates, 1966).

Dockrill, D. W. and R. G. Tanner (eds), *Tradition and Traditions* (Auckland, NZ: University of Auckland Press, 1994).

Ebeling, G., *The Word of God and Tradition*, trans. S. H. Hooke (London: Collins, 1968; German orig. 1964).

Gaybba, B., *The Tradition: An Ecumenical Breakthrough? (A Study of a Faith and Order Study)* (Rome: Herder, 1971).

Geiselmann, J. R., *The Meaning of Tradition*, trans. W. J. O'Hara (Freiburg im Breisgau: Herder, 1966).

Hagen, K., *The Quadrilog: Tradition and the Future of Ecumenism* (Collegeville, MN: Liturgical Press, 1994).

Hobsbawm, E. J. and T. Ranger, *The Invention of Tradition* (Cambridge: Cambridge University Press, 1992).

Holmes, S. R., *Listening to the Past: The Place of Tradition in Theology* (Grand Rapids, MI: Baker Academic, 2002).

Hughes, G. J., *Fidelity without Fundamentalism: A Dialogue with Tradition* (London: Darton, Longman & Todd, 2010).

Kappen, S., *Tradition, Modernity, Counterculture: An Asian Perspective*, 2nd edn (Bangalore: Visthar, 1998).

Kasper, W., *Die Lehre der Tradition in der Römischen Schule* (Freiburg im Breisgau: Herder, 1962).

Kelly, J. F. (ed.), *Perspectives on Tradition and Scripture* (Notre Dame, IN: Fides, 1976).

Langan, T., *The Catholic Tradition* (Columbia, MO: University of Missouri Press, 1998).

Lanne, E., *Tradition et communion des églises* (Leuven: Leuven University Press, 1997).

Lengsfeld, P., 'Tradition innerhalb der konstitutiven Zeit der Offenbarung', in J. Feiner and M. Löhrer (eds), *Mysterium Salutis*, i, *Die Grundlagen heilsgeschtlichen Dogmatik* (Einsiedeln: Benziger, 1965), 239–88.

Lengsfeld, P., 'Tradition und Heilige Schrift in ihr Verhältnis', in J. Feiner and M. Löhrer (eds), *Mysterium Salutis*, i, *Die Grundlagen heilsgeschtlichen Dogmatik* (Einsiedeln: Benziger, 1965), 463–96.

Mackey, J. P., *The Modern Theology of Tradition* (London: Darton, Longman & Todd, 1962).

Mackey, J. P., *Tradition and Change in the Church* (Dublin: Gill, 1968).

Marshall, D. (ed.), *Tradition and Modernity: Christian and Muslim Perspectives* (Washington, DC: Georgetown University Press, 2012).

Newman, Blessed John Henry, *An Essay on the Development of Christian Doctrine* (London: James Toovey, 1845).

Noonan, J. T., *The Church that Can and Cannot Change: The Development of Catholic Moral Teaching* (Notre Dame, IN: University of Notre Dame Press, 2005).

O'Collins, G., *Christology: A Biblical, Historical, and Systematic Study of Jesus*, 2nd edn (Oxford: Oxford University Press, 2009).

O'Collins, G. and D. Braithwaite, 'Tradition as Collective Memory: A Theological Task to be Tackled', *Theological Studies* 76 (2015), 20–42.

Orji, C., 'Does a Hermeneutical Clarification of "Presence" Advance O'Collins' Christology?', *New Blackfriars* 98 (2017), 653–75.

Pelikan, J., *The Christian Tradition: A History of the Development of Doctrine*, 4 vols (Chicago: University of Chicago Press, 1971–89).

Pelikan, J., *Credo: Historical and Theological Guide to Creeds and Confessions of Faith in the Christian Tradition* (New Haven, CT: Yale University Press, 2003).

Pottmeyer, H. J., 'Normen, Kriterien, und Strukturen der Überlieferung', *HFTh*, iv, 124–52.

Pottmeyer, H. J., 'Tradition', in R. Latourelle and R. Fisichella (eds), *Dictionary of Fundamental Theology* (New York: Crossroad, 1994), 1119–24.

Rahner, K. and J. Ratzinger, *Revelation and Tradition*, trans. W. J. O'Hara (London: Burns & Oates, 1966).

Rasmussen, T., 'Tradition', in H. J. Hillerbrand (ed.), *The Oxford Encyclopedia of the Reformation*, iv (New York: Oxford University Press, 1996), 166–9.

Ratzinger, J., *Principles of Catholic Tradition: Building Stones for a Fundamental Theology*, trans. F. McCarthy (San Francisco: Ignatius Press, 1987).

Rodger, P. C. and L. Vischer (eds), *The Fourth World Conference of Faith and Order: Montreal 1963* (London: SCM Press, 1964).

Rösel, M. et al., 'Tradition', *TRE*, xxiii, 689–732.

Rush, O., *The Eyes of Faith: The Sense of the Faithful and the Church's Reception of Revelation* (Washington, DC: Catholic University of America Press, 2009).

Shils, E. A., *Tradition* (London: Faber and Faber, 1980).

Skillrud, H. C., J. F. Stafford, and D. F. Martensen (eds), *Scripture and Tradition* (Minneapolis: Fortress Augsburg, 1995).

Thiel, J. E., *Senses of Tradition: Continuity and Development in Catholic Faith* (New York: Oxford University Press, 2000).

Thiel, J. E., 'The Analogy of Tradition: Method and Theological Judgment', *Theological Studies* 66 (2005), 358–80.

Tilley, W. T., *Inventing Catholic Tradition* (Maryknoll, NY: Orbis, 2000).

Valliere, P., 'Tradition', in L. Jones (ed.), *Encyclopedia of Religion*, 2nd edn, xvi (Detroit: Thomson Gale, 2005), 9267–81.

Vanhoozer, K. J., 'Scripture and Tradition', in K. J. Vanhoozer (ed.), *The Cambridge Companion to Postmodern Theology* (Cambridge: Cambridge University Press, 2003), 149–69.

Wayte, S. R., 'Towards a Christology of Presence', unpublished doctoral thesis for the University of Divinity (Melbourne), 2017.

Wiederkehr, D., 'Das Prinzip der Überlieferung', *HFTh*, iv, 100–23.

Wiederkehr, D., *Wie geschieht Tradition? Überlieferung im Lebensprozess der Kirche* (Freiburg im Breisgau: Herder, 1991).

Wilde, M., *Vatican II: A Sociological Analysis of Religious Change* (Princeton, NJ: Princeton University Press, 2007).

Williams, A. N., 'Tradition', in J. Webster, K. Tanner, and I. Torrance (eds), *Oxford Handbook of Systematic Theology* (Oxford: Oxford University Press, 2007), 362–77.

Williams, D. H., *Retrieving Tradition and Renewing Evangelicalism: A Primer for Suspicious Protestants* (Grand Rapids, MI: Eerdmans, 1999).

Williams, D. H. (ed.), *Tradition, Scripture, and Interpretation: A Sourcebook of the Ancient Church* (Grand Rapids, MI: Baker Academic, 2006).

Williams, M. A., C. Cox, and M. S. Jaffee, *Innovation in Religious Traditions: Essays in the Interpretation of Religious Change* (Berlin: Walter de Gruyter, 1992).

Index of Names

Tilley, W. T. 141
Tillich, P. 9–10
Torrance, I. 141
Torrance, T. 100
Tyndale, W. 69–70

Valliere, P. 22 n., 25, 141
Vanhoozer, K. J. 141
Velati, M. 108 n.
Venantius Fortunatus 80
Vincent de Paul, St 71–2
Vischer, L. 2 n., 141
Visser, M. 67 n.
Vokes, F. E. 77 n.
Voogt, P. de 4 n.
Vorgrimler, H. 90 n.

Ward, G. 32
Wayte, S. R. 141
Webb, D. 94 n.
Webster, J. 141

Weinsheimer, J. 10 n., 47 n.
Wengert, T. J. 63 n.
Wesley, C. 48
Westermeyer, P. 63 n.
Wickham, C. 126 n., 127–30, 134 n.
Wicks, J. 12 n.
Wiederkehr, D. 126 n., 141
Wilde, M. 141
Wilkins, J. 102 n., 105 n.
Wilkinson, J. 62 n.
Williams, A. N. 141
Williams, D. H. 141
Williams, M. A. 141
Williams, R. 77 n.
Wold, B. G. 127 n.
Woodrow, A. N. 11 n., 125 n., 139
Woolf, R. 80 n.
Wren, B. 48

Yeago, D. S. 83 n.
Yeats, W. B. 46